Couples Therapy Workbook

30 | Guided Conversations
To Re-Connect Relationships

Kathleen Mates-Youngman M.A. LMFT

"What a unique resource! A treasure-trove of guided conversations to increase intimacy and friendship. Therapists often ask me for good homework assignments. This book does the thinking for you. Keep it on hand and whether its values, sex, conflict or other challenging issues, you'll have a ready-made way to help your clients make immediate progress."

Ellyn Bader, Ph.D
Founder/Director The Couples Institute

"This is a valuable resource for anyone working with couples. Any couple can profit greatly if they are willing to take Kathleen Youngman's challenge to explore these important topics and discuss these wonderful questions."

Milan and Kay Yerkovich
Authors of best-selling *How We Love series*

Copyright © 2014 by Kathleen Mates-Youngman

Published by
PESI Publishing & Media
PESI, Inc
3839 White Ave
Eau Claire, WI 54703

Cover Design: Documation
Layout: Bookmasters
Editing: Marietta Whittlesey

Printed in the United States of America

ISBN: 978-1-937661-46-5

PESI
Publishing
& Media
www.pesipublishing.com

I dedicate this book to my first love and lifelong love Edward.
Together we have learned and practiced what it is to be safe,
cared for and connected as a couple and a family. Thank you!

Table of Contents

WEEK 3

WEEK 4

About the Author

I was born in Montreal, Canada in 1960 and have always been fascinated by human nature and more specifically romantic relationships. As a teenager in the 1970's I observed a steady cultural shift from the "Ozzie and Harriett" 50's, to the onset of feminist views in the 60's, and the gradual acceptance of divorce as an option in the 70's. I observed some couples clinging to the belief that marriage must be "until death do us part," others struggling with lonely, unhappy marriages, and a general societal angst and tension due to differing views of what it "should" mean to be a man, woman, mother, father, husband and wife.

At the age of 16 my parents were one of the earliest couples to decide to separate and then later divorce. I experienced many reactions from people around me, some supportive, some curious, and some seemingly upset and frightened at the thought that divorce was becoming a viable option. This experience had a profound effect on me as I wondered what differed between the relationships of happy, resilient couples and those that did not survive.

I moved through the restructuring of our family and went on to college to study Fashion Design and Fine Arts. I then moved to California with my future husband and worked as a Fashion Designer, Impressionist Landscape Painter and Art Teacher over the next 14 years. During that time we lived together three years, married, and then became parents of three wonderful children.

Over those years I remained very curious about relationship dynamics. Why were we able to enjoy our marriage and navigate through the challenging times and yet my parents and many other couples were unable to? This nagging curiosity led me back to University to study Psychology and then on to become a Licensed Marriage and Family Therapist specializing in Couples Therapy.

As a couples therapist I have spent thousands of hours working with couples that were distressed, discouraged and most importantly disconnected. We explore their personal history and the history of the relationship and begin to piece together the reasons that the emotional and physical intimacy began to decline and help them to rebuild an empathic, safe, fulfilling and connected relationship.

I feel so blessed to have had my lifelong fascination with relationships come full circle, and be able to offer my experience and expertise to couples in distress and guide them back to a state of healthy, intimate connection!

Introduction for Clinicians

The Inspiration for This Book

I am sure as clinicians working with couples you would agree that the most common complaints you hear are: "We are so disconnected," and "we just don't communicate." They most likely report that the relationship started off quite well but gradually life began to get busier and each partner began to give less attention to nurturing the relationship. Less nurturing meant less emotional and physical intimacy, which resulted in more irritation with each other and the more irritated the couple became with each other, the less likely it was for them to communicate and connect. Once a couple finds themselves in this vicious cycle, as perhaps many of the couples you treat do, it's difficult for them to find their way out on their own.

What I like to do early on is assign the task of spending 20-30 minutes a day together, alone and undistracted, with the goal of improving connection. I encourage clients to do this in the evening after dinner, dishes and any childcare is completed and to develop this as a ritual that includes such things as having a cup of tea, putting on relaxing music and lighting a candle to set the stage for a mindful, calming experience. They are directed to avoid topics that might produce any tension or conflict and to focus instead on sharing words of appreciation, feelings about the relationship, their life in general, or dreams for their future, as well as what they have done recently to make the other feel cared for and valued.

I found that over and over, couples would report back that they struggled with what to discuss during the 20-30 minutes and they would therefore avoid the assignment and become more discouraged about their relationship. As a result, I decided to write *Couples Therapy Workbook: 30 Guided Conversations To Re-Connect Relationships*, a book of thirty connection-building conversations for a couple to have over thirty days. Each day the couple reads a brief description of a topic and why it is relevant to relationship health and then takes turns asking one another a series of ten questions that will guide them through a conversation about the topic. Topics vary in emotional intensity and are all presented in a reader-friendly, non-judgmental and safe manner. The three overall goals of the conversations are: to eliminate any anxiety about what they should discuss by assigning a specific topic each day, to educate couples about important aspects of healthy relationships through the various topics and to improve feelings of emotional, spiritual and physical connection through the actual experience of sharing time and feelings with each other.

Perhaps many of the couples you treat feel stuck in their relationships, or they feel bored, or they feel like their partner has changed to the point that they don't recognize him or her. My work is so gratifying because I've seen couples go through the worst and come out closer than ever. And I usually credit that rebound with two things: (1) an openness and willingness to change and, (2) making a commitment to carve out the time to reconnect, which is where this book comes in.

How This Book is Unique

Couples Therapy Workbook is designed to give your clients tools and a framework with which they can have meaningful conversations about a wide-range of issues and reflect on the strengths of their relationship and the areas that need improvement. It consists of 30 topics and conversations for your couples to have over 30 days or longer, that are then processed with you, the clinician, at the following sessions. The book is arranged into four parts, one week per part, with a short introduction for each week about the goal of those particular conversations and a recap of the topics at the end of each week.

Although many books on the market focus on relationships, I have not found one that focuses strictly on conversation topics for couples, presented in a clear, concise and mindful manner. This book offers topics that are relevant to all relationships and combines a psycho-educational component with a workbook component in the form of specific questions that guide the conversations. The topics presented have not been randomly chosen, but are taken from empirically-based research on marital/relationship health.

My goal in writing *Couples Therapy Workbook* is to help clinicians educate couples about healthy relationships in an enjoyable, manageable and informative way, that not only benefits them from a content perspective but from an experiential perspective as well.

How to Use This Book

You will begin the process by describing to your clients the ritual that they will be asked to create each day to set the stage for a connecting conversation. The ritual requires that your couple join together at the same time each night (perhaps right after dinner or right before bedtime), listen to soothing background music, enjoy a cup of tea, and, most importantly, keep an open, loving, non-judgmental state of mind. Each week you will share with them the theme for the upcoming week and the topics of the conversations they will have. You will emphasize the importance of being open, respectful and present as they have these conversations in order to make this an opportunity to connect, share and learn about each other. It is helpful to have them make a few notes about what they shared and learned after the 30 minutes to bring in to the next session. And finally ask them each to give you a number on a scale of 1 to 10 that describes how connected they feel to the other.

At the following session you will process:

- how easy or difficult it was to create and follow the daily ritual
- how it felt to share their answers

- whether anything was particularly difficult to discuss
- what they learned about themselves and each other.

And once again ask them each again to give you a number on a scale of 1 to 10 that describes how connected they feel to the other.

Important note about this journey: Although this book is structured to be completed in 30 days, it is just as beneficial to take longer if necessary. It is important to use your clinical judgment to determine the timing that will best suit each couple you are treating.

Overview of the Themes for the Four Weeks

Who Are We? Exploring Who We are as a Couple

The conversations in the first week include: Falling in Love; Friendship; Caring. and Affection; Acceptance; Empathy; Emotional Intimacy; Rituals.

During the first week of conversations, your couples reminisce about falling in love, remember what it was like to be best friends, how they easily showed each other care, affection, acceptance and empathy, how they enjoyed sweet rituals and willingly made time for physical intimacy and fun.

Who Am I? Exploring Who Each of You is and What You Bring to the Relationship

The conversations in the second week include: Childhood; Family of Origin Roles; Temperament; Influences; Spirituality; Values; How I Think.

During the second week of conversations, your couples reflect on the culture in their family of origin and the role they developed in the family. They learn about their individual temperaments, talk about the people who have had an influence on them, what role spirituality plays in their life and what they each value. They learn about how they think, so that they can challenge their distorted thoughts and assumptions that get in the way of the relationship.

How Do We Work? Exploring the Dynamics of Our Relationship

The conversations in the third week include: How We Communicate; Conflict; Defensiveness; Sexual Intimacy; Trust; Fidelity and Boundaries; Parenting; Staying in Sync.

During the third week of conversations, your couples learn about any blocks they may have to healthy communication, how to handle conflict in a respectful and constructive way, how to let go of defensiveness so they can really hear their partner; They learn how to talk about their sexual intimacy. They discuss all the areas in the relationship that require trust, the importance of understanding how they define fidelity and what the boundaries in the relationship are. They identify any unhealthy interactional styles they engage in so that they can create a more fair, balanced and mature style. They define the traits they believe an ideal parent has.

What Do We Want? Working Together to Strengthen Our Relationship

The conversations in the fourth week include: Romance; Joy and Gratitude; Respect; Apologies. and Forgiveness; Challenges, Setbacks and Loss; Relationship Savings Accounts; Our Life Path: Past, Present and Future; Keeping Connected.

During the fourth week of conversations your couples focus on what they need to strengthen their relationship going forward. They talk about keeping romance alive, engaging in what brings them joy, experiencing gratitude and showing each other respect through words and actions. They learn the importance of apologies and forgiveness, helping each other cope with challenges, setbacks and loss. They come to understand the meaning of making deposits in the relationship savings account, sharing their dreams and goals for the future, addressing what they have learned on the journey this book has taken them on and making a commitment to continue on this healthy, intimate and connected relationship path.

Couples Therapy Booster Session

Couples Therapy Workbook ends with a Booster Session that I suggest you assign to your clients periodically in order for them to revisit the topics from the book and the conversations they had. Once again they will set the stage for a connecting conversation and share with each other their answers to a series of questions that relate to the 30 topics in the book in order to identify and share the efforts they have made to improve the connection, communication, intimacy and passion in their relationship. When you meet with them again you will process the experience and validate the improvements they have made and address any remaining areas that can be improved.

What to Expect

Couples Therapy Workbook will allow you to educate couples about healthy relationships in an enjoyable, manageable and informative way, that not only benefits them from a content perspective but from an experiential perspective as well. For just 30 minutes a day, over the course of 30 days, your clients will have uninterrupted time together to explore their relationship and share genuine, honest thoughts and feelings. After the 30-day *Couples Therapy Workbook*, your clients will feel more passion, more connection and more intimacy than ever before. You can also return to this workbook and the couples therapy workbook booster session, whenever you find them drifting and in need of a connection tune-up.

If your clients are willing to commit 30 minutes a day for 30 days to improve the connection in their relationship, turn the page!

Introduction for Couples

How This Book Will Improve Your Relationship

As a marriage and family therapist specializing in couples therapy for ten years, the complaints that I hear most often are: "We are so disconnected," and "we just don't communicate." As we begin to talk about the relationship, I very often hear that it started off quite well, but gradually life began to get busier and each partner began to give less attention to nurturing the relationship. Less nurturing meant less emotional and physical intimacy, which resulted in more irritation with each other; the more irritated the couple became with each other, the less likely it was for them to communicate and connect. Once a couple finds themselves in this vicious cycle, as perhaps you and your partner do right now, it's difficult to find your way out on your own.

The way I begin to work with my clients is to gather information about the history of the relationship. We discuss how they met, how the courtship was, what traits in each other they fell in love with, what the early months or years were like, when problems began to arise and what those problems were. The next step is to gather information about their family of origin and to explain to them how their upbringing has impacted the lenses and filters through which they experience their world and relationships. I then help each partner understand how they think, how they communicate and how their own temperament and personality impact the relationship.

As the therapy process continues they each develop a greater understanding of themselves and of how they are experienced by their partner. Ideally, this awareness leads them to take responsibility for their part in the relationship issues and to have more respect, empathy and appreciation for the other. All of these improvements lend themselves to a greater sense of connection, which is a crucial cornerstone to a strong and loving relationship.

Perhaps you feel stuck in your relationship, or you feel bored, or you feel like your partner has changed to the point that you don't recognize him or her. Don't give up. My work is so gratifying, because I've seen couples go through the worst and come out closer than ever. And I usually credit that rebound with two things: (1) an openness and willingness to change and, (2) making a commitment to carve out the time to reconnect, which is where this book comes in.

Couples Therapy Workbook: Guided Relationship-Building Conversations for Clinicians and Clients is designed to give you tools and a framework with which to have meaningful conversations about a wide range of issues and reflect on the strengths of your relationship and the areas that need improvement. Each week will focus on a different aspect of your relationship. Week 1: Who Are We? Exploring who we are as a couple; Week 2: Who Am I? Exploring who each of us is and what we bring to the relationship; Week 3: How Do We Work: Exploring the dynamics of our relationship; and Week 4: What Do We Want? Working together to strengthen our relationship. This program will help you improve personal awareness, empathy, understanding and healthy communication which will result in a much greater sense of connection. My husband and I, who have been married 29 years, have used these tools throughout our marriage and found them to be extremely beneficial in sharpening our relationship skills and nurturing our connection.

For just 30 minutes a day, over the course of 30 days, you and your partner will have uninterrupted time together to explore your relationship and share genuine, honest thoughts and feelings. I recommend that you create a ritual where you get together at the same time each night (perhaps right after dinner or right before bedtime), have soothing background music, possibly a cup of tea, and, most importantly are open, respectful, non-judgmental. After the couples therapy workbook, you and your partner will feel more passion, more connection and more intimacy than ever before. You can also return to this book and the couples therapy workbook booster session, whenever you feel yourselves drifting and in need of a connection tune-up.

If you are willing to commit 30 minutes a day for 30 days to improve the connection in your relationship, turn the page!

Connection Ritual

How to Create the "Connection Ritual"

- Set aside 30 minutes in the evening after dinner, dishes and any childcare is completed.
- Prepare a cup of tea or another soothing drink.
- Put on relaxing music.
- Find somewhere comfortable to sit facing each other.
- Dim the lights and light a candle.
- Make sure you are open, respectful and non-judgmental.
- Give each other a hug and a smile.

Begin the next "Couples Therapy Workbook" Conversation.

Who Are We?

Exploring Who We Are as a Couple

Clinician Prep — 1
Falling in Love

1. Explain to your clients the importance of the following topic:

   "The topic of the first conversation you will have is 'Falling in Love'. Reflecting on the early days of your relationship will remind you of what first attracted you to each other, what traits you admired, how you treated each other, what you enjoyed doing and when you realized you had fallen in love. These memories can help you gain a more balanced view of your partner, motivate you to engage in activities you enjoyed and rekindle those wonderful early feelings of love."

2. Ask them each how connected they currently feel on a scale of 1-10.

   1_____10

3. Review the ritual they will create: "At the same time each day, make a pot of tea or another soothing drink and find a comfortable quiet place to sit. Light a candle, give each other a hug and a smile and begin the first conversation."

4. Explain that they will begin the first conversation by reading together the first page of the assignment and then begin the following conversation by taking turns asking each other the 10 questions.

5. Remind them to be open, respectful and non-judgmental.

6. Give them a copy of the following pages for Conversation #1 "Falling in Love."

7. At the following session you will process:
   - how easy or difficult it was to create and follow the daily ritual
   - how it felt to share their answers
   - whether anything was particularly difficult to discuss
   - what they learned about themselves and each other

   And once again ask them each how connected they feel on a scale of 1-10.

   1_____10

Finally, thank the couple for taking time to focus on each other and improve the connection in their relationship.

I Noticed You Noticing Me. . .How We Began

"Ecstasy cannot last, but it can carve a channel for something lasting."

E.M. Forster

Welcome to *Couples Therapy Workbook: Guided Relationship-Building Conversations!* What better place to start than reflecting back on those first days of falling in love with each other. When you look back on those early romantic days I'm sure you remember it as a wonderful and exciting time. You probably remember thinking that this new person felt special and different from anyone else you had dated, gradually you began to feel quite infatuated, thinking of them more and more often, felt butterflies in your stomach, seemed to need less sleep, life seemed full of possibilities and you thought obsessively about when you could be together again. This euphoria and energy was not just a result of the wonderful person you were falling in love with but also due to the flood of amphetamine-like compounds in the emotion centers of your brain.

Next you probably remember beginning to feel very calm, comfortable and secure with each other. You began to fit nicely into each other's lives, balancing your daily responsibilities with time together nurturing your relationship. At this point your brain was actually producing oxytocin "the cuddle hormone"-that helped you both feel very devoted and attached to each other. You may have decided to live together at that point or become engaged and began to plan a future together.

Over time, however, it's possible that you and your partner, like many couples I have worked with, have found that your relationship sometimes feels less fulfilling and passionate than it used to. That may be one of the reasons you decided to read this book. If so, I would encourage you to take time to reminisce about what you each fell in love with about the other person and find ways to make things feel new and exciting again. Doing this can help you recapture those early feelings of infatuation and romance and can actually produce amphetamines and endorphins in your brain. As a result you will both be reminded of why you became attached to each other and chose to have a future together. This first conversation focuses on your memories of falling in love, in order to create greater feelings of connection and renewed excitement.

Make a pot of tea or another soothing drink and find a comfortable quiet place to sit. Light a candle, give each other a hug and a smile and begin the first conversation.

Couple Conversation — 1
Falling in Love

Take turns asking each other the following questions:

1. Do you remember the first time we met?
2. What was the first thing you noticed about me?
3. What were your first impressions of me?
4. When did you know you had fallen in love with me?
5. Do you remember who said, "I love you" first?
6. What was it about me that you fell in love with?
7. What are the things that you love most about me now?
8. When do you feel closest to me now?
9. Do I show you often enough that I still love you?
10. What can we do to make our relationship feel new and exciting?

Now give each other a hug and a thank you for taking time to focus on each other and improve the connection in your relationship.

1. Explain to your clients the importance of the following topic:

   "The topic of the second conversation you will have is 'Friendship'. It's important to think about the quality of your friendship, as it is a key foundational component in your relationship. If you have a healthy friendship, you are more likely to feel positively about your relationship and manage difficult times."

2. Ask them each how connected they currently feel on a scale of 1-10.

   1_____10

3. Review the ritual they will create: "At the same time each day, make a pot of tea or another soothing drink and find a comfortable quiet place to sit. Light a candle, give each other a hug and a smile and begin the second conversation."

4. Explain that they will begin the second conversation by reading together the first page of the assignment and then begin the following conversation by taking turns asking each other the 10 questions.

5. Remind them to be open, respectful and non-judgmental.

6. Give them a copy of the following pages for Conversation #2 "Friendship."

7. At the following session you will process:
   - how easy or difficult it was to create and follow the daily ritual
   - how it felt to share their answers
   - whether anything was particularly difficult to discuss
   - what they learned about themselves and each other

   And once again ask them each how connected they feel on a scale of 1-10.

   1_____10

Finally, thank the couple for taking time to focus on each other and improve the connection in their relationship.

I Know You Love Me But Are You My Friend?

"It is not a lack of love but a lack of friendship that makes unhappy marriages."

Friedrick Nietzsche

Do you consider your partner your friend? Believe it or not, when I ask this question in a session I often receive blank stares back at me. I am sure that at the beginning of your relationship you did think of your partner as a friend, maybe even your new best friend. You probably noted all sorts of wonderful things about each other, couldn't wait to hear about each other's day, laughed at each other's jokes, easily found common ground and eagerly compromised when it came to making a decision about what movie to see or what restaurant to have dinner at. If you have continued to feel like good friends you are very fortunate, as friendship is a key foundational component of a healthy relationship. You most likely see your relationship in a very positive light and although like every other couple, you irritate each other at times, you are able to let go of anger and move on.

If you do not think of each other as friends but instead as spouses, co-parents, financial partners etc. you probably find that you treat each other with less respect and consideration than you do your actual friends and that you often feel your emotional needs are not being met. When I meet with a couple who does not feel they have a healthy friendship, they are more likely to be easily annoyed with each other and much less likely to make it a priority to spend quality time together nurturing their connection. The following conversation focuses on the traits that create a healthy friendship in order to strengthen the friendship in your relationship.

Make a pot of tea or another soothing drink and find a comfortable quiet place to sit. Light a candle, give each other a hug and a smile and begin the next conversation.

Couple Conversation — 2
Friendship

Take turns asking each other the following questions:
1. Do you think I make spending time with you a priority?
2. Do I show enough interest in your activities?
3. Do you think that I am able to consider your point of view and make compromises?
4. Do I treat you with enough respect and consideration?
5. Are you able to share you likes, dislikes, hopes and dreams with me?
6. Are you ever hurt by the things I say to you?
7. Do I act like I value what you bring to my life?
8. Are you able to have as much fun with me as you do with your friends?
9. Do I tell you often enough how much I appreciate your friendship?
10. How can I be a better friend to you?

Now give each other a hug and a thank you for taking time to focus on each other and improve the connection in your relationship.

Clinician Prep — 3
Caring and Affection

1. Explain to your clients the importance of the following topic:

   "The topic of the third conversation you will have is: 'Caring and Affection'. It's important to think about how you each feel loved and cared for and how much effort you make to be affectionate with one another. Nurturing the care and affection will result in greater appreciation and closeness in your relationship."

2. Ask them each how connected they currently feel on a scale of 1-10.

   1_____10

3. Review the ritual they will create: "At the same time each day, make a pot of tea or another soothing drink and find a comfortable quiet place to sit. Light a candle, give each other a hug and a smile and begin the third conversation."

4. Explain that they will begin the third conversation by reading together the first page of the assignment and then begin the following conversation by taking turns asking each other the 10 questions.

5. Remind them to be open, respectful and non-judgmental.

6. Give them a copy of the following pages for Conversation #3 "Caring and Affection."

7. At the following session you will process:
   • how easy or difficult it was to create and follow the daily ritual
   • how it felt to share their answers
   • whether anything was particularly difficult to discuss
   • what they learned about themselves and each other

   And once again ask them each how connected they feel on a scale of 1-10.

   1_____10

Finally, thank the couple for taking time to focus on each other and improve the connection in their relationship.

How do I Care For You. . .Let Me Count The Ways

*"It's curious how, when you're in love, you yearn to go
about doing acts of kindness to everybody."*

P.G. Wodehouse

It is a universal human need to feel loved. I'm sure that early on in your relationship you found it effortless to show your partner love with words, actions and physical affection, but as time went on, and life got busier, you may have begun to take each other for granted. In order to create a long-lasting relationship, love needs to be thought of not only as a feeling but also a behavior. In other words, love is not just something you feel, but something that you show through actions. It is important not to assume that your partner can read your mind or know what is in your heart. What you *do* is essential to communicating your love. Also, you may not each feel loved and cared for the same way, therefore it is important to ask your partner what does make them feel that way so that you can be sure to show your love in a way that is uniquely special to them.

An excellent way to create connection and emotional security in your relationship is to take time each day to consider what you can do to convey your love to your partner and then checking in to make sure they felt loved and cared for. It may be as simple as calling on your way home from work to see if your partner needs anything from the grocery store for dinner, or getting up early to care for the kids so your partner can sleep in. I have often seen in my practice that when couples take the time to do this, they are rewarded with great appreciation and closeness. The following conversation focuses on how you and your partner experienced love and affection in your family of origin, how you experience it currently and how you can continue to nurture it in your relationship going forward.

Make a pot of tea or another soothing drink and find a comfortable quiet place to sit. Light a candle, give each other a hug and a smile and begin the next conversation.

Caring and Affection

Take turns asking each other the following questions:

1. Did your family openly express affection?
2. Were your parents affectionate with each other?
3. How did you feel cared for as a child?
4. Did your parents tell you they loved you?
5. Am I affectionate enough with you?
6. When was the last time I made you feel cared for?
7. Do you like me to tell you I love you every day?
8. Do you like me to give you gifts?
9. How important are compliments from me?
10. Are you willing to make a commitment to do something daily to show me you love and care for me?

Now give each other a hug and a thank you for taking time to focus on each other and improve the connection in your relationship.

Clinician Prep — 4
Acceptance

1. Explain to your clients the importance of the following topic:

   "The topic of the fourth conversation you will have is 'Acceptance'. It's important to think about how well you accept each other for who you are. Understanding that you each have strengths and weaknesses will allow you to keep a more balanced view of each other and to feel safe to be your authentic self in the relationship."

2. Ask them each how connected they currently feel on a scale of 1-10.

   1_____10

3. Review the ritual they will create: "At the same time each day, make a pot of tea or another soothing drink and find a comfortable quiet place to sit. Light a candle, give each other a hug and a smile and begin the fourth conversation."

4. Explain that they will begin the fourth conversation by reading together the first page of the assignment and then begin the following conversation by taking turns asking each other the 10 questions.

5. Remind them to be open, respectful and non-judgmental.

6. Give them a copy of the following pages for Conversation #4 "Acceptance."

7. At the following session you will process:
   • how easy or difficult it was to create and follow the daily ritual
   • how it felt to share their answers
   • whether anything was particularly difficult to discuss
   • what they learned about themselves and each other

   And once again ask them each how connected they feel on a scale of 1-10.

   1_____10

Finally, thank the couple for taking time to focus on each other and improve the connection in their relationship.

The Beauty of Imperfection

"The greatest happiness of life is the conviction that we are loved — loved for ourselves, or rather, in spite of ourselves."

Victor Hugo

The root of the word "accept" is the Latin term for "receive." When we accept someone for who they are, we are truly receiving them in our hearts. At the beginning of your relationship you most likely found it easy to overlook your partner's flaws and might even have found them charming. As time went on perhaps, these charming flaws have become really annoying to you and gradually even a serious issue. Over time you may have found yourself using the words "always" or "never" to describe your partner. For instance you may say, "you never make plans for us," or "you are always late for dinner." Unfortunately, these types of generalizations can result in your partner feeling that love and acceptance has become very conditional in your relationship and one or both of you are apt to begin to pull away emotionally.

I explain to the couples I work with that for every trait you were originally drawn to in your partner there is generally a flip-side which will be more visible at times of conflict or distress. For instance your "spontaneous" partner may seem unreliable at times, or your "organized" partner may suddenly seem controlling. The more you keep this in perspective the more you will be able to accept the annoyances and soon enjoy again the traits you love. The more accepting you are of each other, the safer it will feel to be vulnerable and the more emotionally intimate your relationship will be. The following conversation focuses on how well you each tolerate strengths and weaknesses in yourselves and each other and on creating a greater sense of acceptance in your relationship.

Make a pot of tea or another soothing drink and find a comfortable quiet place to sit. Light a candle, give each other a hug and a smile and begin the next conversation.

Couple Conversation — 4
Acceptance

Take turns asking each other the following questions:

1. Is it easy or difficult for you to admit to having weaknesses?
2. Do you feel you can be yourself with me?
3. Does it feel safe to be weak or vulnerable with me?
4. Do you feel I love and accept you unconditionally?
5. Do you feel accepted by me more than you feel disapproved of?
6. Do you feel that I notice more what you do right than what you do wrong?
7. Is it easy to approach me about my weaknesses or things I do wrong?
8. If the things that you bother you about me never change will you still be ok with me?
9. Do you feel that I am as accepting of you now as I was early in our relationship?
10. Is there anything that I can do to improve the feelings of acceptance in our relationship?

Now, give each other a hug and a thank you for taking time to focus on each other and improve the connection in your relationship.

1. Explain to your clients the importance of the following topic:

   "The topic of the fifth conversation you will have is 'Empathy'. Having empathy for each other means that you are able to let go of your point of view for a moment and really tune in to how your partner is feeling. It's important to talk about how well you each feel understood in order to create an emotionally safe and connected relationship."

2. Ask them each how connected they currently feel on a scale of 1-10.

   1_____10

3. Review the ritual they will create: "At the same time each day, make a pot of tea or another soothing drink and find a comfortable quiet place to sit. Light a candle, give each other a hug and a smile and begin the fifth conversation."

4. Explain that they will begin the fifth conversation by reading together the first page of the assignment and then begin the following conversation by taking turns asking each other the 10 questions.

5. Remind them to be open, respectful and non-judgmental.

6. Give them a copy of the following pages for Conversation #5 "Empathy."

7. At the following session you will process:
   • how easy or difficult it was to create and follow the daily ritual
   • how it felt to share their answers
   • whether anything was particularly difficult to discuss
   • what they learned about themselves and each other

   And once again ask them each how connected they feel on a scale of 1-10.

   1_____10

Finally, thank the couple for taking time to focus on each other and improve the connection in their relationship.

Couple Conversation — 5
Empathy

Do You Know What I'm Feeling?

"The best and most beautiful things in the world cannot be seen or even touched. They must be felt with the heart."

Helen Keller

At our core, we all want to be understood. We are often willing to agree to disagree if, and that's a big if, we believe we have been heard, and our feelings have been respected. I often see couples engaging in "I'm right and you're wrong" conversations, eyes rolling, arms crossed, staring in opposite directions with an invisible bridge burned between them. Yet, when I softly and gently point out the emotional pain and need I see beneath the frosty surface complaints, a slow thaw often begins. "What I think I'm hearing from you Sally is that you fear your needs will never be a priority to John just like they so seldom were when you were growing up and John you feel that whenever you have tried it doesn't seem to be enough and you are so scared of being criticized like you were as a little boy that you just give up." Bodies begin to shift toward each other, some eye contact is made, eyes moisten and an emotionally honest conversation begins. When a couple can go to this emotionally open place, they are more able to relinquish their point of view for a moment and to show each other empathy.

Empathy is a tuning-in process. It is an attempt by each of you to understand what the other is feeling. I am sure you can think of a time at the beginning of your relationship when you were upset and just needed to be comforted. Your partner was most likely very interested in understanding what you were feeling without judging you, correcting you, or criticizing you, which only deepened your love. The following conversation focuses on how to show empathy to one another as you did early on in order to create an emotionally safe and intimately connected relationship going forward.

Make a pot of tea or another soothing drink and find a comfortable quiet place to sit. Light a candle, give each other a hug and a smile and begin the next conversation.

Couple Conversation — 5
Empathy

Take turns asking each other the following questions:

1. What is your first memory of being upset as a child?
2. Did anyone comfort you?
3. Was it acceptable to experience feelings as a child?
4. If not, which ones were acceptable and which were not?
5. Did you see your parents express a wide range of feelings?
6. Did you ever see your parents comfort each other?
7. Do you feel embarrassed to have or share any feelings?
8. What do need most from me when you feel upset?
9. Do you feel safe to share all of your feelings with me?
10. Do you think that I share my feelings enough?

Now give each other a hug and a thank you for taking time to focus on each other and improve the connection in your relationship.

Clinician Prep — 6
Emotional Intimacy

1. Explain to your clients the importance of the following topic:

   "The topic of the sixth conversation you will have is 'Emotional Intimacy'. Emotional intimacy is the closeness that you experience when you feel supported in exploring your personal growth and safe to share your authentic self emotionally, physically and spiritually. It's important for you to talk about the emotional intimacy in your relationship so that you can be sure to balance being separate individuals with maintaining healthy connection in your relationship."

2. Ask them each how connected they currently feel on a scale of 1-10.

   1_____10

3. Review the ritual they will create: "At the same time each day, make a pot of tea or another soothing drink and find a comfortable quiet place to sit. Light a candle, give each other a hug and a smile and begin the sixth conversation."

4. Explain that they will begin the sixth conversation by reading together the first page of the assignment and then begin the following conversation by taking turns asking each other the 10 questions.

5. Remind them to be open, respectful and non-judgmental.

6. Give them a copy of the following pages for Conversation #6 "Emotional Intimacy."

7. At the following session you will process:
   • how easy or difficult it was to create and follow the daily ritual
   • how it felt to share their answers
   • whether anything was particularly difficult to discuss
   • what they learned about themselves and each other

   And once again ask them each how connected they feel on a scale of 1-10.

   1_____10

Finally, thank the couple for taking time to focus on each other and improve the connection in their relationship.

Couple Conversation — 6
Emotional Intimacy

I'm into You, Are You into Me?

"Passion is the quickest to develop and the quickest to fade.
Intimacy develops more slowly and commitment more gradually still."

Robert Sternberg

I'm sure that when you think back on the early days of your relationship you were able to relate to the "you had me at hello" statement that Dorothy makes to Jerry in the movie "Jerry Maguire." You can recognize that experience of emotional and physical tunnel vision, being magnetically drawn to each other and feeling that time was suspended when you were together. As intoxicating and awesome as those feelings were, they were not the same as experiencing true emotional intimacy. Emotional intimacy develops over time as you and your partner learn to balance being separate individuals with maintaining a connection to each other. As you develop a healthy sense of "I" and "we," you are able to respect and even value your similarities and differences.

I have worked with couples who have become so disconnected that they live very independent parallel lives in the same home and focus only on their individual worlds. These couples often describe the relationship as being very lonely and feel more like roommates than romantic partners. At other times I have had couples come into my office that have become so dependent on each other that they have lost a sense of their own individual identity and feel that there is a void in their lives. If your relationship is healthy you will experience an interdependence that allows you to balance depending on yourself with being vulnerable and depending on your partner.

Clients often ask what it means to be connected. I explain that romantic connection involves caring for one another and sharing enjoyable experiences as you would with a friend, but also—and crucially important—is feeling and expressing a desire to be together and nurturing the sensual/sexual part of the relationship. All of these are important dimensions of emotional intimacy. I have found that once a couple understands how important all of these aspects are, they are able to attend to each aspect individually and experience an overall enhancement of intimacy.

When you have a healthy sense of self, you are able to accept your strengths, weaknesses and imperfections without believing you must change to be loved by your partner or that you must change or "fix" your partner to fit your needs. When you believe you can be who you really are in your relationship and treat your partner with the same respect, you are able to be vulnerable enough to form a relationship that is emotionally and physically intimate. The following conversation focuses on nurturing your romantic connection in order to create greater emotional intimacy in your relationship.

Make a pot of tea or another soothing drink and find a comfortable quiet place to sit. Light a candle, give each other a hug and a smile and begin the next conversation.

Couple Conversation — 6
Emotional Intimacy

Take turns asking each other the following questions:

1. How do you define emotional intimacy?
2. How comfortable are you being emotionally intimate with me?
3. Do you feel like I miss you when we are apart?
4. Are you comfortable spending time without me?
5. Do I ever make you feel guilty for spending time alone or with your friends?
6. Do you think we have enough fun in our relationship?
7. Do you feel connected to me even we are doing things separately?
8. Do you think we spend enough time talking about our feelings, hopes and dreams?
9. Do you think I am affectionate and make our sexual life enough of a priority?
10. Is there anything I can do to improve the emotional intimacy in our relationship?

Now give each other a hug and a thank you for taking time to focus on each other and improve the connection in your relationship.

1. Explain to your clients the importance of the following topic:

   "The topic of the seventh conversation you will have is 'Rituals'. Rituals help to create a culture in your relationship and family, mark important events and add a natural flow and momentum to your lives. It's important to talk about the rituals you have or would like to have in order to create and maintain a deeper sense of shared meaning in your relationship."

2. Ask them each how connected they currently feel on a scale of 1-10.

   1_____10

3. Review the ritual they will create: "At the same time each day, make a pot of tea or another soothing drink and find a comfortable quiet place to sit. Light a candle, give each other a hug and a smile and begin the seventh conversation."

4. Explain that they will begin the seventh conversation by reading together the first page of the assignment and then begin the following conversation by taking turns asking each other the 10 questions.

5. Remind them to be open, respectful and non-judgmental.

6. Give them a copy of the following pages for Conversation #7 "Rituals" and the "Week 1 Recap."

7. At the following session you will process:

   • how easy or difficult it was to create and follow the daily ritual

   • how it felt to share their answers

   • whether anything was particularly difficult to discuss

   • what they learned about themselves and each other over the course of the first seven conversations

   And once again ask them each how connected they feel on a scale of 1-10.

   1_____10

Finally, thank the couple for taking time to focus on each other and improve the connection in their relationship.

The Importance of Over and Over

"She wished for it all to happen again. And of course it did, over and over."

Charlotte Zolotow

Rituals create a great sense of connection in your relationship. I'm sure you can think back on early informal rituals such as spending a few moments together in bed each morning talking, or more formal ones, such as preparing special foods together on the holidays. Regardless of where, how and when you celebrated the ritual, you likely found it created a sense of closeness, connection, anticipation and security in your relationship.

Creating and maintaining rituals allows you to form a deeper sense of shared meaning in your relationship. Just as different cultures have their own traditions, rituals that you share as a couple help to create a unique culture within your relationship. Simple daily and weekly rituals create a natural flow and momentum in your lives and larger annual or seasonal celebratory rituals create a sense of excitement and purpose. They help you celebrate joyful events, offer comfort during times of grief or loss, assist in transitioning to new stages on your life path and create lifelong memories.

In my relationship we enjoy a simple ritual of a daily 3-mile morning hike with our two Siberian Huskies while we talk about what we will be doing in the day ahead. This ritual creates a sense of connection that we take with us through our day until we meet again to share our evening. The following conversation focuses on rituals in your families of origin, rituals that you enjoy in your relationship currently and creating new ones going forward.

Make a pot of tea or another soothing drink and find a comfortable quiet place to sit. Light a candle, give each other a hug and a smile and begin the next conversation.

Couple Conversation — 7
Rituals

Take turns asking each other the following questions:

1. Are rituals important to you?
2. Did your family value rituals?
3. Who was the most active at implementing them?
4. Are there any rituals from your childhood that you would like us to implement?
5. What were holidays, birthdays and other celebrations like growing up?
6. Of the rituals we have, what are your favorites?
7. Do you think it's important to eat dinner together?
8. What do we celebrate?
9. Do you think kissing hello, goodbye and goodnight are important rituals?
10. Would you like to have more rituals in our life together?

Now give each other a hug and a thank you for taking time to focus on each other and improve the connection in your relationship.

Week 1 Recap

Congratulations on completing the seven conversations of Week 1. I hope you enjoyed reminiscing about falling in love and remembering what it was like to be best friends. I hope it felt nice to remember that in the early days you gladly showed each other affection and care, accepted each other for who you were and easily empathized with each other as you shared intimate details of your life. And I hope that it was helpful to remember how well you managed to develop the intimacy in your new relationship by attending to each other's feelings, making time for physical intimacy, finding ways to have fun and developing sweet rituals, while also balancing your own life outside of the relationship. And, mostly I hope that reflecting on the early days of falling in love helped you to feel more connected and hopeful about your relationship than you did a week ago.

And now prepare to begin the conversations in Week 2 that focus on who you each were prior to your relationship and what traits you brought to the relationship. Enjoy.

Who Am I?

Exploring Who Each of You Are,
and What You Bring to the Relationship

Clinician Prep — 8
Childhood

1. Explain to your clients the importance of the following topic:

   "Congratulations, you have now reached the second group of conversations that focus on who you each were prior to your relationship and what traits you brought to the relationship. This group begins with your eighth conversation and the topic is 'Childhood'. Your childhood has a great impact on how you see family and romantic relationships and influences those relationships throughout your lives. It's important to talk about your childhood so that you can know each other better and have greater respect for how you each came to be the people you are today."

2. Ask them each how connected they currently feel on a scale of 1-10.

   1_____10

3. Review the ritual they will create: "At the same time each day, make a pot of tea or another soothing drink and find a comfortable quiet place to sit. Light a candle, give each other a hug and a smile and begin the eighth conversation."

4. Explain that they will begin the eighth conversation by reading together the first page of the assignment and then begin the following conversation by taking turns asking each other the 10 questions.

5. Remind them to be open, respectful and non-judgmental.

6. Give them a copy of the following pages for Conversation #8 "Childhood."

7. At the following session you will process:
   • how easy or difficult it was to create and follow the daily ritual
   • how it felt to share their answers
   • whether anything was particularly difficult to discuss
   • what they learned about themselves and each other

   And once again ask them each how connected they feel on a scale of 1-10.

   1_____10

Finally, thank the couple for taking time to focus on each other and improve the connection in their relationship.

Couple Conversation — 8
Childhood

Nature vs. Nurture

"The family, that dear octopus from whose tentacles we never quite escape, nor, in our innermost hearts, ever quite wish to."

Dodie Smith

A family is much more than a group of people who live in the same home. Although families can take many different forms, they all share certain characteristics that have a huge impact on who you become as an individual and what you expect from life and other relationships. Both you and your partner grew up in a family with its own set of spoken and unspoken rules, expectations, roles, power structure, style of verbal and non-verbal communication, style of showing love and affection, values, priorities and methods of problem-solving. All of these traits combined to form your family culture and was your first experience with relationships. These relationships are based on a shared history and even when they are affected by distance, death, or estrangements, the family influence continues.

When you and your partner met and developed a romantic relationship neither of you came as blank slates but instead as a culmination of your genetic and interpersonal history. If you grew up in families with similar styles it most likely was, or will be, fairly easy to create your own relationship and family culture. If you had quite different childhood experiences it most likely was, or will be, more challenging to navigate the differences in outlook on how a family should be.

After the first therapy session with a couple I schedule a session alone with each of them to learn about their childhoods. The information that I gather is invaluable in helping me to understand why they think, feel and behave the way they do and how these traits impact their relationship. I have seen many couples have "aha" moments as we connect the dots between their experience in their families of origin and how they are in the relationship.

The more you understand about the dynamics of your family of origin and your partner's, the more you will be able to blend together and develop a healthy culture for the family you create. The following conversation focuses on exploring the culture in your families of origin and creating the culture you would like for your relationship and family.

Make a pot of tea or another soothing drink and find a comfortable quiet place to sit. Light a candle, give each other a hug and a smile and begin the next conversation.

Couple Conversation — 8
Childhood

Take turns asking each other the following questions:

1. Do you know much about your parents' upbringing?
2. Did you spend much time with your extended family?
3. Is there a parent you were closer to and/or one that you had more difficulty getting along with?
4. How would you describe your childhood?
5. Do you think our childhoods were similar?
6. Is there any history of mental illness or addiction in your family?
7. How do you feel about spending time with your family? My family?
8. What traits in your family would you like to continue in ours?
9. Are you happy with the relationship I have with your family?
10. How do you think your childhood impacts our relationship and family?

Now give each other a hug and a thank you for taking time to focus on each other and improve the connection in your relationship.

1. Explain to your clients the importance of the following topic:

   "The topic of the ninth conversation you will have is 'Family of Origin Roles'. In your last conversation you talked about the overall culture in your family of origin and how it influenced you. Now you will focus on your role in that family. The role you had was shaped by your birth order, gender, temperament and family dynamics and you brought that part of you into this relationship as well. Understanding how that role plays out in this relationship will give you more information about why you relate to each other the way you do."

2. Ask them each how connected they currently feel on a scale of 1-10.

   1_____10

3. Review the ritual they will create: "At the same time each day, make a pot of tea or another soothing drink and find a comfortable quiet place to sit. Light a candle, give each other a hug and a smile and begin the ninth conversation."

4. Explain that they will begin the ninth conversation by reading together the first page of the assignment and then begin the following conversation by taking turns asking each other the 10 questions.

5. Remind them to be open, respectful and non-judgmental.

6. Give them a copy of the following pages for Conversation #9 "Family of Origin Roles."

7. At the following session you will process:
   • how easy or difficult it was to create and follow the daily ritual
   • how it felt to share their answers
   • whether anything was particularly difficult to discuss
   • what they learned about themselves and each other

   And once again ask them each how connected they feel on a scale of 1-10.

   1_____10

Finally, thank the couple for taking time to focus on each other and improve the connection in their relationship.

Me Before I Became a We

"What greater thing is there for human souls than to feel that they are joined for life, to be with each other in silent unspeakable memories."

George Eliot

You've discussed how the culture in your family of origin has impacted you, well, a big component of that is your role in the family. Just as a group of children playing "house" choose roles and act them out, so did you when you were born into your family of origin. As a member of your family you unconsciously began to develop a style of relating to others that was due in part to your unique personality and to the needs of the family. Your role may have shifted over time if new siblings came along or if there were any other changes to your family structure.

You might have gone from an only child who was doted on to becoming an older sibling who was expected to be the "big girl" or "big boy" and help out when a new baby arrived. You might have been the only one of your gender in a group of siblings or one of several of the same gender. You might have had siblings who were spread out with several years between births or very close together in age, or might have had new step-siblings at some point. Academics, friendships and finding unique talents might have been quite easy for you or you may have struggled with any or all of those things while observing your siblings moving through life with ease. You may have connected well with a parent that had a similar personality and strengths or struggled to find that connection while other siblings were able to.

All of these situations, and many other possible ones, had a great impact on your experience in your family and, of course, in life in general. Your role in your family and your interactions with all family members, was your introduction to socialization and has influenced the way you and your partner relate. The following conversation focuses on your role in your family of origin, what you learned about relationships from those early experiences and how it impacts your relationship currently.

Make a pot of tea or another soothing drink and find a comfortable quiet place to sit. Light a candle, give each other a hug and a smile and begin the next conversation.

Couple Conversation — 9
Family of Origin Roles

Take turns asking each other the following questions:

1. How did your birth order affect your role in the family?

2. Did your parents treat each of you differently?

3. If you were a first-born or only child were you: responsible, perfectionistic, serious?

4. If you were a middle-child were you: even-tempered, mellow, a good negotiator?

5. If you were the youngest were you: social, rebellious, somewhat selfish?

6. How do you think your birth order has affected your life?

7. Were you ever a black-sheep, family clown or acting-out child? If so, why do you think that was?

8. Did your relationship with any of your siblings affect your self-image or self-esteem?

9. Did you ever have to be the "parent" in your family because of a parent that was unavailable for any reason?

10. Do you think your birth order has affected our relationship?

Now give each other a hug and a thank you for taking time to focus on each other and improve the connection in your relationship.

Clinician Prep — 10
Temperament

1. Explain to your clients the importance of the following topic:

"The topic of the tenth conversation you will have is 'Temperament'. You were each born with your own unique temperament and it has a great impact on how you think, feel and behave. Learning about your temperament styles will help you to understand each other and to respect and appreciate your similarities and differences."

2. Ask them each how connected they currently feel on a scale of 1-10.

1_____10

3. Review the ritual they will create: "At the same time each day, make a pot of tea or another soothing drink and find a comfortable quiet place to sit. Light a candle, give each other a hug and a smile and begin the tenth conversation!"

4. Explain that they will begin the tenth conversation by reading together the first page of the assignment and then begin the following conversation by taking turns asking each other the 10 questions.

5. Remind them to be open, respectful and non-judgmental.

6. Give them a copy of the following pages for Conversation #10 "Temperament."

7. At the following session you will process:
- how easy or difficult it was to create and follow the daily ritual
- how it felt to share their answers
- whether anything was particularly difficult to discuss
- what they learned about themselves and each other

And once again ask them each how connected they feel on a scale of 1-10.

1_____10

Finally, thank the couple for taking time to focus on each other and improve the connection in their relationship.

The "Nature," in Nature vs. Nurture

"If a man does not keep pace with his companions, perhaps it is because he hears a different drummer. Let him step to the music which he hears, however measured or far away."

Henry David Thoreau

Although you grew up in the same home with the same parents as your siblings, I am sure you are aware of very distinct differences in your personalities. This is due in part to your birth order and life experiences, but also to your own unique temperament. Your temperament determines how you act and communicate, as well as your attitudes, values and talents.

Your temperament and that of your partners, will determine whether you are an extrovert or an introvert, whether you prefer to experience life intuitively or through experience, whether you make decisions based on logic or how you feel and whether you prefer structure or flexibility. You may also find that one of you lives more in the moment and the other more in the future, one of you is fairly predictable and the other spontaneous, one is easily upset one is not, or one jumps right to problem-solving while the other likes to understand their feelings first.

As a couples therapist, I help my clients to have greater knowledge about their own temperament and that of their partner. It is very important to understand that no style is better or worse to have and to respect and appreciate your differences. Let's face it, your relationship would probably be a little dull if you had exactly the same temperament. The more you understand each other and not just tolerate, but appreciate, your differences the more you will be able to maintain emotional stability in your relationship. The following conversation focuses on understanding and appreciating your temperament styles in order to improve the respect and connection in your relationship.

Make a pot of tea or another soothing drink and find a comfortable quiet place to sit. Light a candle, give each other a hug and a smile and begin the next conversation.

Couple Conversation — 10
Temperament

Take turns asking each other the following questions:

1. Do you prefer to be alone or with others?
2. Do you gather information by paying attention to reality or trusting your intuition?
3. Do you make decisions based on facts or emotion?
4. Do you tend to be structured and firm or flexible and adaptable?
5. When you are stressed, do you need space or to be comforted?
6. Do you like to work first and play later or to combine them?
7. Do you like routine or variety?
8. When you are upset do you make a plan to fix things on your own or do you need to talk to someone?
9. When something happens that I don't like do you think I get upset easily or can I let it go?
10. Do you think that I respect and appreciate our differences?

Now give each other a hug and a thank you for taking time to focus on each other and improve the connection in your relationship.

1. Explain to your clients the importance of the following topic:

   "The topic of the eleventh conversation you will have is 'Influences'. As you moved along your life path the people that you encountered and the experiences that you had have also influenced who you are today. Reflecting back on your life path and sharing your story with your partner is another wonderful way to know yourself and your partner better and to create connection."

2. Ask them each how connected they currently feel on a scale of 1-10.

   1————————————————————10

3. Review the ritual they will create: "At the same time each day, make a pot of tea or another soothing drink and find a comfortable quiet place to sit. Light a candle, give each other a hug and a smile and begin the eleventh conversation."

4. Explain that they will begin the eleventh conversation by reading together the first page of the assignment and then begin the following conversation by taking turns asking each other the 10 questions.

5. Remind them to be open, respectful and non-judgmental.

6. Give them a copy of the following pages for Conversation #11 "Influences."

7. At the following session you will process:
   - how easy or difficult it was to create and follow the daily ritual
   - how it felt to share their answers
   - whether anything was particularly difficult to discuss
   - what they learned about themselves and each other

   And once again ask them each how connected they feel on a scale of 1-10.

   1————————————————————10

Finally, thank the couple for taking time to focus on each other and improve the connection in their relationship.

Couple Conversation — 11
Influences

I Am Who I Am Because Of...

"Blessed is the influence of one true, loving human soul on another."

George Eliot

From the moment of your birth you were influenced by the people around you. You left a warm, supportive womb and entered into a world surrounded by people you depended upon for survival. Your parents set the stage for whether or not you could expect consistent, reliable, care and attention. If they did meet these needs, you developed a positive sense of self-worth and felt safe enough to venture out into your world to discover more. This healthy attachment allowed you the balance of developing your individual personality with a soft place to land if needed.

If you did not experience a healthy early attachment with your parents, there might have been other people in your life that took on the role of primary caregiver. It might have been a caring older sibling, a grandparent, or parent of a friend that offered you quality time and attention, which gave you a sense of self-worth. Either way, as you continued along your path you took in all sorts of information and met many different kinds of people who added to the tapestry of your life-story. You might have been unaware of these influences as they were unconsciously filed away in your psyche, or you might have been very obviously moved by something you saw, heard or felt that changed you in subtle or not so subtle ways. All of these experiences accumulated to form your character, personality and perspective on yourself, your relationships and your life in general. The following conversation focuses on identifying and sharing the many influences you have had in your life so that you can have a greater understanding of how you each became the people you are today.

Make a pot of tea or another soothing drink and find a comfortable quiet place to sit. Light a candle, give each other a hug and a smile and begin the next conversation.

Couple Conversation — 11
Influences

Take turns asking each other the following questions:

1. Who do you think was the greatest influence on how you love? What did you learn from that person?
2. Who had the greatest influence on your self-esteem?
3. Who had the greatest influence on your career choice?
4. Who had the greatest influence on your life goals?
5. Who had the greatest influence on how you parent or want to parent?
6. Who had the greatest influence on the type of friend you are?
7. Who had the greatest influence on how you handle stress and challenges?
8. Have I influenced you in any way?
9. Who have you admired most in your life?
10. Other than me, who are you most grateful for in your life?

Now give each other a hug and a thank you for taking time to focus on each other and improve the connection in your relationship.

Clinician Prep — 12
Spirituality

1. Explain to your clients the importance of the following topic:

   "The topic of the twelfth conversation you will have is 'Spirituality'. Sharing your definition of spirituality and any impact it has had on your life, will allow you to talk about if and how you would like to incorporate it into your relationship. It's important to understand that spirituality is very individual and to discuss it openly and respectfully."

2. Ask them each how connected they currently feel on a scale of 1-10.

   1_____10

3. Review the ritual they will create: "At the same time each day, make a pot of tea or another soothing drink and find a comfortable quiet place to sit. Light a candle, give each other a hug and a smile and begin the twelfth conversation."

4. Explain that they will begin the twelfth conversation by reading together the first page of the assignment and then begin the following conversation by taking turns asking each other the 10 questions.

5. Remind them to be open, respectful and non-judgmental.

6. Give them a copy of the following pages for Conversation #12 "Spirituality."

7. At the following session you will process:
   • how easy or difficult it was to create and follow the daily ritual
   • how it felt to share their answers
   • whether anything was particularly difficult to discuss
   • what they learned about themselves and each other

   And once again ask them each how connected they feel on a scale of 1-10.

   1_____10

Finally, thank the couple for taking time to focus on each other and improve the connection in their relationship.

The Quest For An Authentic And Fulfilling Life

"The function of prayer is not to influence God, but rather to change the nature of the one who prays."

Soren Kierkegaard

Generally speaking, spirituality focuses on a journey of self-discovery and finding meaning, purpose and direction in one's life. For some, a sense of spirituality comes from organized religion with its tradition, doctrine and rituals. For them, it feels natural and fulfilling, while for others the focus on the relationship between themselves and something larger seems more fitting. For many, spirituality offers a means to balance work and relationships and a way to remain whole and centered with all the distractions and trials of life.

You and your partner may share the same religious background and spiritual beliefs or you may have had very different experiences. You may have decided long ago that you must have a partner who shares your spiritual beliefs or you may have been open to having a partner with different views. It might also be that the role of spirituality in your life has changed over time therefore it is ideal to have an open dialogue about this with your partner. In my work I have found that many couples enjoy the ritual of a religious practice and find that it can be very bonding and offer support during difficult times. Whether a couple has similar or differing beliefs, what matters most is for each partner to feel safe to share their spiritual views, to know they will be respected and to determine if and how they will incorporate spirituality into their relationship and family culture.

Awareness of your beliefs, who you are at your core, what your journey has been and what you would like it to be going forward is essential to connecting to your partner. Sharing this journey and search for meaning and purpose with your significant other is a gift to you both and an incredibly humbling and connecting experience. The following conversation focuses on exploring your spiritual beliefs and the role of spirituality in your relationship.

Make a pot of tea or another soothing drink and find a comfortable quiet place to sit. Light a candle, give each other a hug and a smile and begin the next conversation.

Couple Conversation — 12
Spirituality

1. Did your family practice any particular religion?

2. If so, do you think it added to family connectedness?

3. How would you define spirituality?

4. Do you think it is or has been important for us to practice a religion or incorporate spirituality into our lives?

5. If we have or will have children do you want religion or spirituality to be a part of our family culture?

6. Have there been times in your life that you have been particularly spiritual?

7. Have there been times in your life when spirituality has helped?

8. Are you tolerant of others' spiritual/religious beliefs?

9. Do you find me tolerant of others spiritual/religious beliefs?

10. What do these words mean to you:
    - purpose
    - mindful
    - truth
    - love
    - God
    - higher power
    - prayer
    - meditation
    - suffering

Now give each other a hug and a thank you for taking time to focus on each other and improve the connection in your relationship.

1. Explain to your clients the importance of the following topic:

   "The topic of the thirteenth conversation you will have is 'Values'. It's very important to think about what you value so you can be sure to incorporate those things into your life. The more awareness you have of each other's values, the more you will be able to find balance and purpose in your life and relationship."

2. Ask them each how connected they currently feel on a scale of 1-10.

   1_____10

3. Review the ritual they will create: "At the same time each day, make a pot of tea or another soothing drink and find a comfortable quiet place to sit. Light a candle, give each other a hug and a smile and begin the thirteenth conversation."

4. Explain that they will begin the thirteenth conversation by reading together the first page of the assignment and then begin the following conversation by taking turns asking each other the 10 questions.

5. Remind them to be open, respectful and non-judgmental.

6. Give them a copy of the following pages for Conversation #13 "Values."

7. At the following session you will process:
   • how easy or difficult it was to create and follow the daily ritual
   • how it felt to share their answers
   • whether anything was particularly difficult to discuss
   • what they learned about themselves and each other

   And once again ask them each how connected they feel on a scale of 1-10.

   1_____10

Finally, thank the couple for taking time to focus on each other and improve the connection in their relationship.

Couple Conversation — 13
Values

Who We Are at Our Core

*"The most important ingredient we put into any relationship
is not what we say or do, but what we are."*

Stephen Covey

Values are things that matter to you and that guide the way you live and work. Awareness of your personal values provides you with an internal reference point for what you have decided is good, important, useful and beautiful for you and, in turn, drives your behavior. I have worked with many couples who may differ greatly in what they like to do in their spare time and yet still feel close and connected because they share the same core values. For instance, one may love skydiving or riding motorcycles and the other may prefer to stay home with a good book and a cup of tea, yet they both value family, friends and spirituality, therefore feel they are connected and living a meaningful life together.

Unfortunately, with the busyness of life, it is all too easy to lose sight of what you truly value and what brings you joy. You may find that you have become so focused on accomplishing things, completing the never-ending to-do lists, or pleasing others, that you are feeling depleted and out of balance. It is extremely beneficial to slow down periodically and revisit your core values. Although it might not be possible to incorporate all that you value into your life at all times, awareness of what those values are can keep you from feeling that your life is empty and lacking purpose. The following conversation focuses on identifying what you each value, where you are similar, where you differ and how to create a healthy balance of values in your life together.

Make a pot of tea or another soothing drink and find a comfortable quiet place to sit. Light a candle, give each other a hug and a smile and begin the next conversation.

Take turns asking each other the following questions:

1. What do you value most at this point in your life?
2. Do you think that your values have changed as you have grown older?
3. Are there things that you value doing that you aren't able to do at this time?
4. Are your values similar to those of your parents?
5. Do you think we have similar values?
6. Does our relationship allow you the freedom to engage in activities that you value?
7. Are there any values that we don't share that create problems in our relationship?
8. Do you feel that I respect your values?
9. Do you think it's important to model healthy values to our children/future children?
10. Is there anything I can do to help you live a value-driven life?

Now give each other a hug and a thank you for taking time to focus on each other and improve the connection in your relationship.

Clinician Prep — 14
How I Think

1. Explain to your clients the importance of the following topic:

   "The topic of the fourteenth conversation you will have is 'How I Think'. You both have a lens and filter that influence how you experience your relationship and sometimes that results in distorted thinking. This conversation will help you identify the cognitive distortions you engage in so that you can create more accurate and healthy interactions."

2. Ask them each how connected they currently feel on a scale of 1-10.

   1_____10

3. Review the ritual they will create: "At the same time each day, make a pot of tea or another soothing drink and find a comfortable quiet place to sit. Light a candle, give each other a hug and a smile and begin the fourteenth conversation."

4. Explain that they will begin the fourteenth conversation by reading together the first page of the assignment and then begin the following conversation by taking turns asking each other the 10 questions.

5. Remind them to be open, respectful and non-judgmental.

6. Give them a copy of the following pages for Conversation #14 "How I Think" and the "Week 2 Recap."

7. At the following session you will process:
   - how easy or difficult it was to create and follow the daily ritual
   - how it felt to share their answers
   - whether anything was particularly difficult to discuss
   - what they learned about themselves and each other over the course of the second group of conversations.

   And once again ask them each how connected they feel on a scale of 1-10.

   1_____10

Finally, thank the couple for taking time to focus on each other and improve the connection in their relationship.

Perception Becomes Reality

*"We are what we think. All that we are arises with our thoughts.
With our thoughts, we make the world."*

Buddha

Just as children growing up in the same family will often describe their upbringing differently, you and your partner might describe events in your life together in very different ways. As a psychotherapist I often sit with a couple, listening to each partner describe a recent argument with details that differ wildly. I attempt to validate both of their realities, while also making sense of why each of them experienced the situation so differently.

As a child you lived in a family with a unique culture that shaped how you saw yourself and the world. How your parents loved you and how they related to each other and their world shaped the way you saw yourself, your relationships and your world, as you grew up. You gradually developed a lens through which you saw your experiences and filters through which you interpreted these experiences. Your lens and filters continue to influence how you experience your relationship and can lead to assumptions about your partner's feelings and motivations. Unfortunately, these assumptions can be distorted at times and result in conflicts in your relationship.

Aaron Beck Ph.D. first developed the theory behind cognitive distortions in 1976. There have been many different names and descriptions used since then, but these are the ones that I see most often with couples in my practice.

1. **Jumping to Conclusions:** assuming they know what the other is feeling and what their motivations are.

2. **Personalization:** believing that everything the other says and does is a reaction to them.

3. **Control Fallacies:** believing they have total control or no control over the other and the relationship.

4. **Blaming:** holding the other responsible for their pain and the problems in the relationship.

5. Shoulds: having rigid rules about how the other should behave and feel.

6. Global Labeling: generalizing one or two qualities into a negative label of the other.

7. Always Being Right: going to any length to prove they are right.

8. Tunnel Vision: filtering out all the positive aspects of the relationship and focusing only on the negative.

9. Magnification: describing things as worse than they are.

10. Polarized Thinking: things are either "black or white" with no grey areas.

Cognitive distortions can be very damaging to your relationship as these perceptions become your reality and drive your behavior. Ideally you need to become aware of what your default thought process is in order to shift it when necessary. To do this you must be willing to ask yourself how much evidence, if any, there is for your thoughts and to consider a more accurate and balanced way of looking at things. The following conversation focuses on identifying the cognitive distortions you use, in order to improve your interactions.

Make a pot of tea or another soothing drink and find a comfortable quiet place to sit. Light a candle, give each other a hug and a smile and begin the next conversation.

Take turns asking each other the following questions:

1. Which of the ten cognitive distortions listed on the previous page do you think I engage in?

2. Is there any one in particular that I use often?

3. Can you think of an example of when I did so recently?

4. How does my distorted thinking make you feel?

5. Have you ever tried to challenge my assumptions about you?

6. If so, was I open to listening to you?

7. Do you think my distorted thinking has affected our connection at times?

8. Have you ever been hurt by a cognitive distortion I have used?

9. If so which one is most hurtful to you?

10. Would you be willing to point out when I am making distorted assumption about you if I promise to be open-minded?

Now give each other a hug and a thank you for taking time to focus on each other and improve the connection in your relationship.

Week 2 Recap

Congratulations on completing the conversations of week two. I hope you found it interesting to reflect on the culture in your family of origin and the role you developed in your family. I hope that understanding the rules, expectations, values and style of showing love in each of your families helped you to think about a blend that would represent who you are as a couple. I hope that you also enjoyed talking about the people who have had an influence on you, what role spirituality plays in your life and what you value. As you did this, I hope that you learned a little more about each other and were able to respect your differences and appreciate your similarities. And I hope it was helpful to learn more about your temperament as it determines some very basic and important things about yourself, and also how you think so that you can challenge your distorted thoughts when they get in the way. And, mostly, I hope that learning more about who each of you is and what you bring to the relationship helped you to feel more connected and hopeful about your relationship than you did a week ago.

And now prepare to begin the conversations in week 3 that focus on exploring the dynamics in your relationship. Enjoy.

How Do We Work?

Exploring the Dynamics of Our Relationship

1. Explain to your clients the importance of the following topic:

   "Congratulations, you have now reached the third group of conversations, which focus on exploring the dynamics of your relationship. This group begins with your fifteenth conversation and the topic is 'How We Communicate'. When you try to communicate you may find that you don't feel heard, that you misunderstand each other, or that the conversation becomes tense or conflictual. Understanding any blocks to healthy communication you have will enable you to listen well, respond respectfully and feel closer."

2. Ask them each how connected they currently feel on a scale of 1-10.

   1_____10

3. Review the ritual they will create: "At the same time each day, make a pot of tea or another soothing drink and find a comfortable quiet place to sit. Light a candle, give each other a hug and a smile and begin the fifteenth conversation."

4. Explain that they will begin the fifteenth conversation by reading together the first page of the assignment and then begin the following conversation by taking turns asking each other the 10 questions.

5. Remind them to be open, respectful and non-judgmental.

6. Give them a copy of the following pages for Conversation #15 "How We Communicate."

7. At the following session you will process:
   • how easy or difficult it was to create and follow the daily ritual
   • how it felt to share their answers
   • whether anything was particularly difficult to discuss
   • what they learned about themselves and each other

   And once again ask them each how connected they feel on a scale of 1-10.

   1_____10

Finally, thank the couple for taking time to focus on each other and improve the connection in their relationship.

Couple Conversation — 15
How We Communicate

We Hear Each Other But Are We Listening?

"The problem with communication is the illusion it has occurred."

George Bernard Shaw

In the ten years that I have been working as a couple's therapist, the most common goal I hear from a couple in a first session is to improve communication. They often state that they don't feel listened to or understood. As we begin to explore their communication style I generally find that the problem lies in how they send and/or receive messages. Hearing is not listening. We can all hear things without really listening, but when we really pay attention to what we hear we are truly listening.

I am sure that like most couples you have had the experience of telling your partner something only to ask, "are you listening to me?" Often the response is, "yes of course I'm listening, you said. . ." and, of course, having your words regurgitated back to you tells you that you were heard but does not necessarily mean you were listened to. For instance, in a session I might hear one partner say, "I was telling Robert how stressed out I am about finances right now and he kept reading the paper." Then Robert responds, "Yes Susan and when you asked if I was listening I said, yes, I heard you say you were stressed out about money." I then ask Susan how she would have liked Robert to respond and she says, "I would have liked it if he had put the paper down and looked at me while I was speaking so that I would know he was really listening and cared about how I feel." There are numerous blocks to healthy, productive communication and in this case Robert blocked it by not making eye contact and appearing distracted. Unfortunately, as a result Susan did not feel listened to, validated or connected to Robert.

Other problems can arise because of how a message is interpreted. For instance, in a session Robert might share, "I asked Susan if it was ok for me to golf on Saturday, and she clearly wasn't ok with that." And then Susan responds, "I don't know what you're talking about. I said it was fine." I then ask Robert what made him think she wasn't okay with it, and he responds, "Well she gave me this really curt answer and walked away so it was clear she wasn't ok with it." In a case like this I would explore whether or not Robert interpreted Susan correctly. She might have really meant it was fine, and he assumed otherwise, or she might have said one thing and felt another which was conveyed by her tone, attitude, facial expressions and actions.

If your words are not in line with what you convey non-verbally, or your partner misinterprets what is heard, you risk creating resentment and frustration, which can lead to a disconnect in your relationship. The following conversation focuses on identifying any blocks you have to effective communication in order to ensure it's clear, effective and healthy.

Make a pot of tea or another soothing drink and find a comfortable quiet place to sit. Light a candle, give each other a hug and a smile and begin the next conversation.

Couple Conversation — 15
How We Communicate

Take turns asking each other the following questions:

1. Do you ever feel that I am argumentative regardless of what you bring up?

2. Do you ever feel that I just tune you out?

3. Do I ever change the subject or make a joke when you are speaking?

4. Do you ever feel that I am thinking about what I am going to say next instead of really listening?

5. When we are arguing do I bring up issues from the past instead of focusing on the present?

6. Does it seem like I always have to be right?

7. Do I ever jump in and give you advice while you are speaking?

8. Do I ever misinterpret what you are saying and insist you mean something else?

9. Do you ever feel like I'm judging you while you speak?

10. Do I ever seem to agree with you just to change the subject or make everything ok?

Now give each other a hug and a thank you for taking time to focus on each other and improve the connection in your relationship.

1. Explain to your clients the importance of the following topic:

   "The topic of the sixteenth conversation you will have is 'Conflict'. All couples have conflict, but some are able to remain respectful while others attack each other with critical, judgmental and contemptuous words. Addressing how you cope with conflict in your relationship will help you to do so in a constructive and caring manner."

2. Ask them each how connected they currently feel on a scale of 1-10.

   1_____10

3. Review the ritual they will create: "At the same time each day, make a pot of tea or another soothing drink and find a comfortable quiet place to sit. Light a candle, give each other a hug and a smile and begin the sixteenth conversation."

4. Explain that they will begin the sixteenth conversation by reading together the first page of the assignment and then begin the following conversation by taking turns asking each other the 10 questions.

5. Remind them to be open, respectful and non-judgmental.

6. Give them a copy of the following pages for Conversation #16 "Conflict."

7. At the following session you will process:
   • how easy or difficult it was to create and follow the daily ritual
   • how it felt to share their answers
   • whether anything was particularly difficult to discuss
   • what they learned about themselves and each other

   And once again ask them each how connected they feel on a scale of 1-10.

   1_____10

Finally, thank the couple for taking time to focus on each other and improve the connection in their relationship.

Couple Conversation — 16
Conflict

"I'm Right You're Wrong" to
"Maybe We Are Both a Little Bit Right."

"Peace is not the absence of conflict, but the ability to cope with it."

Unknown

Conflict is an unavoidable part of any relationship. The key is to be able to handle a conflict with a healthy attitude and in a constructive manner. If you think about a recent conflict you had with your partner, would you say you were able to express your thoughts and feelings respectfully, without becoming critical and mean? Did you listen to your partner's point of view and find a way to stay calm and compromise? And afterward did you each say or do something that demonstrated your love and care for each other? If so, you have been successful in managing conflict without harming your relationship. In contrast, if you became judgmental, critical or contemptuous, you most likely found that you did not accomplish anything positive but instead chipped away at any closeness and connection in your relationship. You will feel that kind of conflict in your heart and in your gut if the messages you get from your partner are: "I'm right and you're wrong," "I am more powerful" and, "I have no interest in your point of view."

Unfortunately, I find in my practice that many couples are unaware of the difference between a complaint, a critical comment and, worse yet, a contemptuous comment. A complaint simply expresses to your partner that you are unhappy about something, whereas a criticism expresses that you disapprove of them, and contempt communicates that you think they are worthless. Needless to say, feeling disapproved of or worthless is very destructive to a relationship. The following is an example of one partner expressing that they are unhappy that the other partner has not helped with the dishes. Read each one and note the difference between a complaint, a criticism and contempt.

Complaint: *Honey, I'm disappointed that you haven't offered to help me with the dishes all week.*

Criticism: *It's been really selfish of you not to help me with the dishes all week.*

Contempt: *As usual, you've been selfish and lazy all week and haven't even noticed all the work I do around here.*

The following conversation focuses on understanding the difference between a complaint, a criticism and contempt, in order to create a respectful and constructive approach to dealing with conflict in your relationship.

Make a pot of tea or another soothing drink and find a comfortable quiet place to sit. Light a candle, give each other a hug and a smile and begin the next conversation.

Couple Conversation — 16
Conflict

Take turns asking each other the following questions:

1. When we have a conflict do you ever find me disrespectful?

2. Have I ever made you feel stupid, worthless or disapproved of?

3. Would you say that I am able to stay calm when we have conflict or that I escalate easily?

4. Do you ever feel that I am judging you?

5. Do you find that I listen to your point of view or do I jump in quickly with my opinion?

6. Are you able to express a complaint or make a request without my getting upset?

7. Do you think that we generally resolve things well?

8. Do you think that we are good at having a conflict and then calming down and feeling close again?

9. Do you think that having a conflict has ever helped us make positive changes in our relationship?

10. Is there anything I can do to make our conflicts less difficult?

Now give each other a hug and a thank you for taking time to focus on each other and improve the connection in your relationship.

Clinician Prep — 17
Defensiveness

1. Explain to your clients the importance of the following topic:

   "The topic of the seventeenth conversation you will have is 'Defensiveness'. In the previous conversation you discussed how to have conflict without attacking each other, but there may still be times when you experience your partner's comments as attacks and become defensive. Unfortunately, defensiveness sabotages communication, therefore once you are aware of the defense mechanism you use, you will be able to avoid doing so and instead hear your partner, feel your feelings and express them in a clear and respectful manner."

2. Ask them each how connected they currently feel on a scale of 1-10.

   1_____10

3. Review the ritual they will create: "At the same time each day, make a pot of tea or another soothing drink and find a comfortable quiet place to sit. Light a candle, give each other a hug and a smile and begin the seventeenth conversation."

4. Explain that they will begin the seventeenth conversation by reading together the first page of the assignment and then begin the following conversation by taking turns asking each other the 10 questions.

5. Remind them to be open, respectful and non-judgmental.

6. Give them a copy of the following pages for Conversation #17 "Defensiveness."

7. At the following session you will process:
   • how easy or difficult it was to create and follow the daily ritual
   • how it felt to share their answers
   • whether anything was particularly difficult to discuss
   • what they learned about themselves and each other

   And once again ask them each how connected they feel on a scale of 1-10.

   1_____10

Finally, thank the couple for taking time to focus on each other and improve the connection in their relationship.

Must We Be on Guard, or Can We Drop The Swords?

*"What counts in making a happy marriage is not so much how
compatible we are, but how we deal with incompatibility."*

Daniel Goleman

In the last conversation you talked about how to conflict without attacking each other with critical or contemptuous comments. Now we will address what can happen if you do feel attacked. It is perfectly natural that you do whatever you can to avoid emotional or physical pain. Just as you would run for cover if you saw a bear along a hiking trail, you will find a way to run for cover if you sense the emotional threat of an attack from your partner. In order to protect yourself you are likely to use one or more of three types of defense mechanisms: avoidance, denial and/or acting out.

For example, let's say your partner is upset that you forgot about a date night that was planned. If avoidance is your defense mechanism you might just change the subject. With denial you might insist that you were never told about the date night. And if you act out you might get really angry and accuse your partner of never being happy about anything. In each of these examples your defensiveness is an attempt to keep from feeling something uncomfortable or emotionally painful such as, "I'm a terrible partner," or, "I can't ever make my partner happy."

Although these defensive behaviors might make you feel emotionally safe in the moment, they actually sabotage any hope of closeness, growth and connection in your relationship. It may be that you are actually being attacked or it may only be your perception, but ideally you should be able to hear what your partner is saying, tolerate any uncomfortable feelings that come up and address the situation respectfully.

Although you may use different defense mechanisms in different situations, you will generally use one that was modeled in your family of origin. The following conversation focuses on identifying the defense mechanism you typically use so that you can let go of that and, instead, really hear your partner, feel your feelings and express them in a clear and respectful manner.

Make a pot of tea or another soothing drink and find a comfortable quiet place to sit. Light a candle, give each other a hug and a smile and begin the next conversation.

Take turns asking each other the following questions:

1. When you bring things up to me do I ever *avoid* you by getting quiet, ignoring you, or distracting myself with things like TV, food or shopping?

2. Do I ever *deny* there is a problem by acting like nothing happened, doing something to change your mood, or by not following through on the things you ask of me?

3. When we have a problem do I ever *act-out* by becoming argumentative right away, criticizing you, or becoming demanding?

4. Has the defense mechanism that I use ever hurt you?

5. Have you ever tried to point these behaviors out to me?

6. Has my defensiveness kept us from resolving certain issues in our relationship?

7. In order to reduce my defensiveness, would you be open to my letting you know if I feel attacked?

8. Do you ever feel attacked by me when we have conflict?

9. If so do you think that you use the defense mechanisms of *avoidance*, *denial* or *acting-out*?

10. Is there something that I can do to help you hear me without feeling attacked?

Now give each other a hug and a thank you for taking time to focus on each other and improve the connection in your relationship.

1. Explain to your clients the importance of the following topic:

   "The topic of the eighteenth conversation you will have is 'Sexual Intimacy'. As with many other aspects of your relationship, the sexual intimacy you share will evolve over time and requires attention and effort. It is important to have a conversation about your sexual relationship so that you can make it a priority to keep it open, fun and satisfying."

2. Ask them each how connected they currently feel on a scale of 1-10.

   1_____10

3. Review the ritual they will create: "At the same time each day, make a pot of tea or another soothing drink and find a comfortable quiet place to sit. Light a candle, give each other a hug and a smile and begin the eighteenth conversation."

4. Explain that they will begin the eighteenth conversation by reading together the first page of the assignment and then begin the following conversation by taking turns asking each other the 10 questions.

5. Remind them to be open, respectful and non-judgmental.

6. Give them a copy of the following pages for Conversation #18 "Sexual Intimacy."

7. At the following session you will process:
   - how easy or difficult it was to create and follow the daily ritual
   - how it felt to share their answers
   - whether anything was particularly difficult to discuss
   - what they learned about themselves and each other

   And once again ask them each how connected they feel on a scale of 1-10.

   1_____10

Finally, thank the couple for taking time to focus on each other and improve the connection in their relationship.

My Way, Your Way, Our Way

"There is no keener pleasure than that of bodily love."

Plato

Sexual styles are as unique as each person in a relationship. Although sexual intimacy differentiates a friendship from a romantic relationship, you and your partner may differ in your experience with sex and your expectation for sex in your relationship. The sexual intimacy you share will evolve over the course of your relationship due to developmental stages you go through, life stressors and physical changes. The key to maintaining a healthy sexual relationship is for you to clearly communicate your needs and desires and for each of you to remain non-judgmental and open.

It is extremely important for each of you to understand that there is no right or wrong way to be sexual. Your personality will have a lot to do with your sexual style, and it will most likely evolve and change over time. Although you have certainly seen the Hollywood version of sexual passion, it is important to have realistic expectations, to be open to exploring different ways of expressing yourself sexually and to nurture the sexual chemistry in your relationship.

One of the first symptoms of disconnection in a relationship is a decline in sexual interactions. Couples who don't feel emotionally close don't want to be sexually close. I hear over and over from couples who they just don't have the time or energy for sex. Generally what has happened is that nurturing the romance has become less of a priority, unhealthy conflict then increases and, as a result, the desire to be sexual declines. The following conversation focuses on the sexual intimacy in your relationship and creating ways to make it a priority to nurture it and keep it open, fun and satisfying.

Make a pot of tea or another soothing drink and find a comfortable quiet place to sit. Light a candle, give each other a hug and a smile and begin the next conversation.

Couple Conversation — 18
Sexual Intimacy

Take turns asking each other the following questions:

1. Do you think that we have a healthy sexual life?
2. Do you feel comfortable talking to me about sex?
3. Is there anything I could do to make it more comfortable?
4. Do you think our sexual relationship has changed over time?
5. If so, is it better or worse?
6. Is there anything you would like to do differently in our sexual life?
7. Did your parents discuss sex with you growing up?
8. How did you feel about sex growing up?
9. How important is sex to you in our relationship?
10. Am I respectful of your sexual needs?

Now give each other a hug and a thank you for taking time to focus on each other and improve the connection in your relationship.

Clinician Prep — 19
Trust

1. Explain to your clients the importance of the following topic:

   "The topic of the nineteenth conversation you will have is 'Trust'. There are many areas in your relationship where trust is an essential component. Having a conversation about what those areas are and how well you do trust each other in those areas, will create a greater sense of safety and connection."

2. Ask them each how connected they currently feel on a scale of 1-10.

   1_____10

3. Review the ritual they will create: "At the same time each day, make a pot of tea or another soothing drink and find a comfortable quiet place to sit. Light a candle, give each other a hug and a smile and begin the nineteenth conversation."

4. Explain that they will begin the nineteenth conversation by reading together the first page of the assignment and then begin the following conversation by taking turns asking each other the 10 questions.

5. Remind them to be open, respectful and non-judgmental.

6. Give them a copy of the following pages for Conversation #19 "Trust."

7. At the following session you will process:
   • how easy or difficult it was to create and follow the daily ritual
   • how it felt to share their answers
   • whether anything was particularly difficult to discuss
   • what they learned about themselves and each other

   And once again ask them each how connected they feel on a scale of 1-10.

   1_____10

Finally, thank the couple for taking time to focus on each other and improve the connection in their relationship.

Couple Conversation — 19
Trust

You Have My Back And I'll Have Yours!

*"The highest compact we can make with our fellow is,
let there be truth between us forevermore."*

Ralph Waldo Emerson

When you think of trust in your relationship you likely think in terms of fidelity, yet there are many other areas in your relationship where trust is involved. To begin with, in order to fall in love you needed to trust that your heart would be treated tenderly as you exposed your innermost vulnerabilities. Over time you shared intimate details of your life and needed to trust that this information would remain private and never be used against you. Once you began sharing a home and finances, or began to think about doing so, you needed to trust that neither would be misused and that you would have transparency with one another. The more you experience each other as emotionally and physically available, respectful of the relationship boundaries and supportive of each other's needs, feelings, and time, the greater sense of trust you will have in each other and in the relationship.

The trust you have in your partner can be betrayed in many ways. Whether it's forgetting plans that were important to you, sharing something embarrassing about you, or failing to disclose money spent, you will always feel wounded. In my practice I have seen that addiction, abuse and emotional or physical infidelity have the most devastating impacts on trust. In these situations, it is extremely difficult, if not impossible, to fully regain the trust that was betrayed. The following conversation focuses on exploring the trust in your relationship and creating and maintaining a high degree of it going forward.

Make a pot of tea or another soothing drink and find a comfortable quiet place to sit. Light a candle, give each other a hug and a smile and begin the next conversation.

Couple Conversation — 19
Trust

Take turns asking each other the following questions:

1. Can you trust me to keep a secret?
2. Do you think I keep my promises?
3. Am I able to remain serious and supportive when you share very vulnerable feelings?
4. Do you trust me when we are apart?
5. Do you trust that I don't criticize you to others?
6. Do you trust me with our finances?
7. Do you trust me to make things that are important to you a priority?
8. Do you trust that I will not abuse you or our present or future children?
9. Do you trust that I won't abuse substances?
10. Do you trust me to respect our home and belongings

Now give each other a hug and a thank you for taking time to focus on each other and improve the connection in your relationship.

Fidelity and Boundaries

1. Explain to your clients the importance of the following topic:

"The topic of the twentieth conversation you will have is 'Fidelity and Boundaries'. In the previous conversation, you discussed trust. A large component of trust is agreeing upon how you define fidelity and what boundaries you need in your relationship. Having a conversation about what you need those limits to be, and promising to stay within those limits, will strengthen the security and connection in your relationship."

2. Ask them each how connected they currently feel on a scale of 1-10.

1_____10

3. Review the ritual they will create: "At the same time each day, make a pot of tea or another soothing drink and find a comfortable quiet place to sit. Light a candle, give each other a hug and a smile and begin the twentieth conversation."

4. Explain that they will begin the twentieth conversation by reading together the first page of the assignment and then begin the following conversation by taking turns asking each other the 10 questions.

5. Remind them to be open, respectful and non-judgmental.

6. Give them a copy of the following pages for Conversation #20 "Fidelity and Boundaries."

7. At the following session you will process:
- how easy or difficult it was to create and follow the daily ritual
- how it felt to share their answers
- whether anything was particularly difficult to discuss
- what they learned about themselves and each other

And once again ask them each how connected they feel on a scale of 1-10.

1_____10

Finally, thank the couple for taking time to focus on each other and improve the connection in their relationship.

Affair Prevention For Your Relationship

"Love is the irresistible desire to be irresistibly desired."

Robert Frost

You've had a conversation about the importance of trust in the relationship. One way to establish and maintain trust is to be very clear about your relationship boundaries. You and your partner may wrestle with what it means to be faithful and what is considered a healthy boundary. Does that mean you cannot talk to someone of the opposite sex? That you must not develop friendships with someone of the opposite sex? That you may be friends, but not discuss intimate details about your relationship?

Literally speaking, fidelity is defined as, "strict observance of promises, duties, etc." and boundary is defined as, "something that indicates or fixes a limit or extent." The key words here are: "promises" and "limit." I often say to clients that whatever two consenting adults decide is appropriate for their relationship is all that matters. What is important is to determine and be clear about what your relationship "limit" is and to "promise" not to exceed that limit.

I have worked with many couples who have struggled with the fallout of one partner's violating the promises and limits that the other relied upon. There is always great pain, and if the couple is able to heal it takes a good deal of time. Often these couples had gradually paid less and less attention to the friendship and romance in the relationship, which resulted in less connection and vulnerability to a violation of boundaries. The following conversation focuses on the limits and promises in your relationship in order to create and maintain healthy boundaries.

Make a pot of tea or another soothing drink and find a comfortable quiet place to sit. Light a candle, give each other a hug and a smile and begin the next conversation.

Take turns asking each other the following questions:

1. Are you comfortable with my going out with my friends?
2. Are you comfortable with my going to bars or clubs with my friends?
3. Are you comfortable with my having friends of the opposite sex?
4. Are you comfortable with my sharing intimate details of our lives with a friend of the opposite sex?
5. Do you want me to discuss any spending with you prior to doing so?
6. Are you comfortable with my spending time alone?
7. If we have or will have children, do you think it's important to have couple time away from them?
8. Do you believe we should have transparency with our phones/email/Facebook etc?
9. Are you comfortable with my watching pornography?
10. Do you think that I should feel comfortable saying no to sex if I am not in the mood?

Now give each other a hug and a thank you for taking time to focus on each other and improve the connection in your relationship.

1. Explain to your clients the importance of the following topic:

   "The topic of the twenty-first conversation you will have is 'Parenting'. Whether you are parents now or plan to be in the future, it is important to understand that you may have different parenting styles. Having a conversation about your views on parenting will help you create a respectful, consistent and fulfilling co-parenting experience."

2. Ask them each how connected they currently feel on a scale of 1-10.

   1_____10

3. Review the ritual they will create: "At the same time each day, make a pot of tea or another soothing drink and find a comfortable quiet place to sit. Light a candle, give each other a hug and a smile and begin the twenty-first conversation."

4. Explain that they will begin the twenty-first conversation by reading together the first page of the assignment and then begin the following conversation by taking turns asking each other the 10 questions.

5. Remind them to be open, respectful and non-judgmental.

6. Give them a copy of the following pages for Conversation #21 "Parenting."

7. At the following session you will process:
   • how easy or difficult it was to create and follow the daily ritual
   • how it felt to share their answers
   • whether anything was particularly difficult to discuss
   • what they learned about themselves and each other

   And once again ask them each how connected they feel on a scale of 1-10.

   1_____10

Finally, thank the couple for taking time to focus on each other and improve the connection in their relationship.

Couple Conversation — 21
Parenting

Yours, Mine and Ours

"Everything depends on upbringing."

Leo Tolstoy

Becoming a parent is one of the most definitive stages of life. If you had a happy childhood you are more likely to want to have a family and to parent in a similar style to that of your parents. If your childhood was not a happy one, you may have decided not to have children or to have a very different parenting style from that of your own parents.

Some parents tend to be quite strict; others have few expectations and act more like friends, but ideally parents should be attentive, forgiving and set healthy boundaries and expectations. When I work with parents who have children experiencing behavioral problems, I help them get on the same page and learn how to model respect for each other and the home, to be consistent, reinforce desired behaviors and show empathy.

It is so important to understand that even if you and your partner have similar parenting styles there will be times that you do things differently. If you are planning to have children, it is very beneficial to talk about what traits you believe an ideal parent has. Talking about this in advance will allow you to see where your ideas are similar and where they differ so that you can begin to understand and respect each point of view.

If you are parents already I am sure that there has been a time when you did not see eye to eye on how to parent your child. At times like this it is so important to avoid taking an "I'm right you're wrong" approach, as this will not only hurt and insult your partner but will undermine the connection in your relationship. Ideally, you will remember that you are a team and that you both have the best interests of your child in mind. The more you are able to hear each other's point of view and come to a decision that allows you to be on the same page, the better off your child and your relationship will be. Having a healthy, respectful approach to co-parenting will allow you to keep your communication open and develop an even greater sense of connection and intimacy in your relationship. The following conversation focuses on understanding your parenting styles in order to create a respectful co-parenting experience.

Make a pot of tea or another soothing drink and find a comfortable quiet place to sit. Light a candle, give each other a hug and a smile and begin the next conversation.

Couple Conversation — 21
Parenting

Take turns asking each other the following questions:

1. Do you think it's necessary to be strict and demanding as a parent?
2. Do you think it's important to be nurturing and affectionate?
3. Do you think it's important to explain the reasoning behind our rules?
4. Do you think our children will benefit from clear limits, consistency and natural consequences for their behavior?
5. Do you think it's important to be a good listener?
6. Do you think it's important to attend school events?
7. Do you think our children should be allowed to express an opinion?
8. Do you think our children should have some choices and options?
9. How much supervision do you think children need?
10. How can we have a friendship with our child while also maintaining respect as the parents?

Now give each other a hug and a thank you for taking time to focus on each other and improve the connection in your relationship.

1. Explain to your clients the importance of the following topic:

   "The topic of the twenty-second conversation you will have is 'Staying in Sync'. During conflict or challenging times, some couples are able to remain flexible and connected, while others fall into a more dysfunctional pattern of interaction. Addressing how you interact at those times will help you to create a healthy style that allows you to maintain connection even when things are difficult."

2. Ask them each how connected they currently feel on a scale of 1-10.

   1_____10

3. Review the ritual they will create: "At the same time each day, make a pot of tea or another soothing drink and find a comfortable quiet place to sit. Light a candle, give each other a hug and a smile and begin the twenty-second conversation."

4. Explain that they will begin the twenty-second conversation by reading together the first page of the assignment and then begin the following conversation by taking turns asking each other the 10 questions.

5. Remind them to be open, respectful and non-judgmental.

6. Give them a copy of the following pages for Conversation #22 "Staying in Sync" and the "Week 3 Recap."

7. At the following session you will process:
   • how easy or difficult it was to create and follow the daily ritual
   • how it felt to share their answers
   • whether anything was particularly difficult to discuss
   • what they learned about themselves and each other over the course of the third group of conversations

   And once again ask them each how connected they feel on a scale of 1-10.

   1_____10

Finally, thank the couple for taking time to focus on each other and improve the connection in their relationship.

Couple Conversation — 22
Staying in Sync

What Is The Dance We Do?

"The success of marriage comes not in finding the "right" person, but in the ability of both partners to adjust to the real person they inevitably realized they married."

John Fischer

As discussed in previous conversations, neither of you has come into your relationship as blank slates, but as a culmination of your own temperaments, personalities and histories. Combining your unique traits makes your relationship interesting and can help you to balance each other out, especially during conflict. Who you are as a whole determines your approach to your relationship and results in a dance you do as a couple. The stronger the friendship, respect and communication in your relationship, the more flexible you will be with your part in the dance. Like a beautiful waltz, you are able to glide through your relationship in sync and to be aware of the subtle cues along the way that let you know when small adjustments are necessary to stay balanced and close.

Unfortunately, if you are lacking in certain keys areas of your relationship, you are more likely to be very rigid with each other especially when you disagree, stepping on each other's toes, throwing off the balance and beauty of your dance and sometimes landing flat on your faces. You might even continue to dance your part the same way and expect your partner to change his or her steps. If you push hard enough and long enough you might find that your partner pushes back harder and faster, throwing you off even more or that they just let go and you find yourself spinning around the floor alone.

Couples who have trouble interacting and coping with conflict often fall into one of three types of repetitive, dysfunctional patterns. The first pattern involves a partner who pursues closeness and another who is more comfortable with distance. Unfortunately the pursuer may begin to demand closeness resulting in greater distance, or may eventually give up altogether resulting in disconnection.

The second type are couples who fall into a pattern where one person blames their partner for the conflict, and the other partner placates by doing whatever they can to correct the situation. With this style the blamer is seldom forced to take responsibility for their part in the problem and the placater stuffs their feelings to keep the peace, which often results in depression and disconnection.

The third style involves a partner who "over-functions" by handling most, if not all, of the responsibility in the relationship while the other "under-functions," taking on very little or no responsibility. Although the over-functioning partner may like to be in control, and the under-functioning one may enjoy having things done for him or her, over time resentment can build on both sides.

Each of these unhealthy interactional styles gradually deteriorates the connection in the relationship. The following conversation focuses on exploring your interactions in order to create a fair, balanced and respectful style that will maintain the connection in your relationship.

Make a pot of tea or another soothing drink and find a comfortable quiet place to sit. Light a candle, give each other a hug and a smile and begin the next conversation.

Couple Conversation — 22
Staying in Sync

Take turns asking each other the following questions:

1. When we are having a conflict do we ever engage in the pursuer/distancer dance?

2. If so, do you think I am the one who is uncomfortable with tension and therefore pursues closeness, or do I become distant to avoid the situation?

3. Do you think we ever engage in the blame/placate dance?

4. If so, do you think I am the critical and blaming partner or the one who accepts responsibility just to make things better?

5. Do you think we ever engage in the over-functioning/under-functioning dance?

6. If so, do you think I am the one who likes to take more control and responsibility in our relationship or the one who allows you to do most things?

7. How does my part in the dance affect you?

8. Do you think our couple style during conflict seeps into our everyday dynamic?

9. Do you think our style gets in the way of our connection?

10. What can I do to create a more fair and balanced style during conflict and at any other time?

Now give each other a hug and a thank you for taking time to focus on each other and improve the connection in your relationship.

Week 3 Recap

Congratulations on completing the conversations of Week Three. I hope that you learned about any blocks you have to healthy communication, how to handle conflict in a respectful and constructive way and to let go of any defensiveness so that you can really hear your partner, feel your feelings and express them in a clear and caring manner. I hope that you found it helpful to talk about all the areas in your relationship that require trust, and how important it is to be clear on how you define fidelity and what the boundaries in your relationship are. I hope it was enlightening and fun to learn how you each feel about your sexual intimacy and what you might explore to keep it exciting and new. And, if you are parents or are planning to become parents, I hope you learned a lot about the traits you believe an ideal parent has, what your parenting style is or will be and to respect any differences you have in order to co-parent effectively. Finally, I hope that you were able to identify any unhealthy interactional styles you might engage in so that you can create a fair, balanced and mature style. Overall, I hope that learning more about the dynamics in your relationship helped you to feel more connected and hopeful about your relationship than you did a week ago.

And now prepare to begin the conversations in Week Four that focus on exploring what you each want and how to work together to strengthen your relationship. Enjoy.

What Do We Want?

Working Together to Strengthen Our Relationship

1. Explain to your clients the importance of the following topic:

"Congratulations, you have reached the final group of conversations which focus on exploring what you each want and how to work together to strengthen your relationship. This group begins with your twenty-third conversation and the topic is 'Romance'. I'm sure it was easy for you to be romantic early on in the relationship, but over time you might have put less effort into it and even begun to feel more like roommates. Having a conversation about the romance in your relationship will help you to make it a priority to find ways to keep the spark alive."

2. Ask them each how connected they currently feel on a scale of 1-10.

1————————————————————————————10

3. Review the ritual they will create: "At the same time each day, make a pot of tea or another soothing drink and find a comfortable quiet place to sit. Light a candle, give each other a hug and a smile and begin the twenty-third conversation."

4. Explain that they will begin the twenty-third conversation by reading together the first page of the assignment and then begin the following conversation by taking turns asking each other the 10 questions.

5. Remind them to be open, respectful and non-judgmental.

6. Give them a copy of the following pages for Conversation #23 "Romance."

7. At the following session you will process:
- how easy or difficult it was to create and follow the daily ritual
- how it felt to share their answers
- whether anything was particularly difficult to discuss
- what they learned about themselves and each other

And once again ask them each how connected they feel on a scale of 1-10.

1————————————————————————————10

Finally, thank the couple for taking time to focus on each other and improve the connection in their relationship.

Couple Conversation — 23
Romance

After the Honeymoon Ends

"Men always want to be a woman's first love, women like to be a man's last romance."

Oscar Wilde

Now that you and your partner are feeling more connected again it's time to focus on keeping that connection alive by fanning the spark of romance. I'm sure you remember well how lovely your romance was early on. How natural it seemed to be romantic without any effort or planning. How you longed for each other and how quickly time flew when you were together and how it dragged on when you were apart. As time passed, and responsibilities and distractions got in the way, you likely began to make less effort to plan for romance which resulted in feeling disconnected and less desired.

I have often seen couples who very naturally nurture and maintain the *things* in life that they value. I will hear from them in a session that they cannot find the time for a date night yet they manage to find the time and energy to attend to their homes, cars, gardens and bodies. They sometimes even feel guilty if they take time away from these other things and give it to the relationship, yet they complain that their relationship is lacking romance and connection.

The more you and your partner understand that although nurturing your romance takes effort, it must be a priority, the stronger your friendship and connection will be. The following conversation focuses on the romance in your relationship and creating opportunities to keep the spark alive.

Make a pot of tea or another soothing drink and find a comfortable quiet place to sit. Light a candle, give each other a hug and a smile and begin the next conversation.

Couple Conversation — 23
Romance

Take turns asking each other the following questions:

1. How do you define romance?
2. What is romantic to you?
3. Were your parents romantic?
4. How often do you think we should experience romance?
5. Do you think the romance has changed in our relationship?
6. Do you think we should be equally responsible for creating opportunities for romance?
7. Do you think one of us is more romantic than the other?
8. Do you feel more romantic when we are away from home?
9. What was the last romantic moment you remember us having?
10. What can I do to create more romance in our relationship?

Now give each other a hug and a thank you for taking time to focus on each other and improve the connection in your relationship.

Joy and Gratitude

1. Explain to your clients the importance of the following topic:

   "The topic of the twenty-forth conversation you will have is 'Joy and Gratitude'. Couples who are able to experience joyful moments together and are grateful for each other are more able to tolerate distressing times in life. It is important to talk about what brings you joy, and what you are grateful for, in order to create more opportunity for both in your relationship."

2. Ask them each how connected they currently feel on a scale of 1-10.

   1_____10

3. Review the ritual they will create: "At the same time each day, make a pot of tea or another soothing drink and find a comfortable quiet place to sit. Light a candle, give each other a hug and a smile and begin the twenty-fourth conversation."

4. Explain that they will begin the twenty-forth conversation by reading together the first page of the assignment and then begin the following conversation by taking turns asking each other the 10 questions.

5. Remind them to be open, respectful and non-judgmental.

6. Give them a copy of the following pages for Conversation #24 "Joy and Gratitude."

7. At the following session you will process:
   • how easy or difficult it was to create and follow the daily ritual
   • how it felt to share their answers
   • whether anything was particularly difficult to discuss
   • what they learned about themselves and each other

   And once again ask them each how connected they feel on a scale of 1-10.

   1_____10

Finally, thank the couple for taking time to focus on each other and improve the connection in their relationship.

Don't Worry, Be Happy

"All animals, except for man, know that the principal business of life is to enjoy it."

Samuel Butler

If you were lucky enough to have grown up in a happy home you are most likely able to find joy and gratitude in your life quite easily. As an infant and child you we able to have fun easily, batting at a mobile hanging above your crib, smiling as you mastered rolling over, squealing with joy as you were chased around by mom or dad at bedtime, or playing kick the can with the neighborhood kids. Even as a teenager you most likely sought out friends and fun to balance the stress of homework and studying. Unfortunately as you settled into adulthood you might have begun to believe that you didn't have time to do the things that bring you joy and that it was more important to be productive.

Not only does the lack of joy in your life impact your mood, but it can also keep you from experiencing joy and gratitude in your relationship. I have found in my practice that couples who are able to let go of the to-do list, slow down, and be present, are more able to be grateful for each other and the little things that bring them joy in life and in the relationship. These couples are also more able to tolerate distress, and even a crisis in life, due to the security of knowing that they are in it together.

If you are willing to make the time to engage in what brings you joy, or at least willing to explore what that might be should you not know, it will be a gift to your emotional, spiritual and physical health, as well as to the health of your relationship. The following conversation focuses on what brings each of you joy and how to create more joy and gratitude in your relationship.

Make a pot of tea or another soothing drink and find a comfortable quiet place to sit. Light a candle, give each other a hug and a smile and begin the next conversation.

Couple Conversation — 24
Joy and Gratitude

Take turns asking each other the following questions:

1. What is your most joyful memory as a child?

2. What brings you joy now?

3. Do you think we make enough time for joy in our relationship?

4. Do I make you feel joyful? Why or why not?

5. Do you feel that you have much to be grateful for?

6. What do you feel grateful for?

7. When you look at the world do you see much to be grateful for?

8. Do you find yourself becoming more grateful for people and situations as you get older?

9. Do you think we should set aside time each week to talk about what we are grateful for?

10. Is there anything I can do to help bring more joy and gratitude to our life?

Now give each other a hug and a thank you for taking time to focus on each other and improve the connection in your relationship.

1. Explain to your clients the importance of the following topic:

   "The topic of the twenty-fifth conversation you will have is 'Respect'. When you feel respected by your partner you are able to be your genuine self and you experience a strong sense of friendship and connection. Having a conversation about how respected you each feel will help you to make any improvements that you need and to feel closer and more valued in the relationship."

2. Ask them each how connected they currently feel on a scale of 1-10.

   1＿＿＿＿＿＿＿＿＿＿＿＿＿＿＿＿＿＿＿＿＿10

3. Review the ritual they will create: "At the same time each day, make a pot of tea or another soothing drink and find a comfortable quiet place to sit. Light a candle, give each other a hug and a smile and begin the twenty-fifth conversation."

4. Explain that they will begin the twenty-fifth conversation by reading together the first page of the assignment and then begin the following conversation by taking turns asking each other the 10 questions.

5. Remind them to be open, respectful and non-judgmental.

6. Give them a copy of the following pages for Conversation #25 "Respect."

7. At the following session you will process:
   • how easy or difficult it was to create and follow the daily ritual
   • how it felt to share their answers
   • whether anything was particularly difficult to discuss
   • what they learned about themselves and each other

   And once again ask them each how connected they feel on a scale of 1-10.

   1＿＿＿＿＿＿＿＿＿＿＿＿＿＿＿＿＿＿＿＿＿10

Finally, thank the couple for taking time to focus on each other and improve the connection in their relationship.

Couple Conversation — 25
Respect

Respecting Each Other = Respecting the Relationship

"You should respect each other and refrain from disputes; you should not,
like water and oil, repel each other, but should, like milk and water, mingle together."

Buddha (Prince Gautama Siddharta)

Respect is a cornerstone of a healthy, strong, connected relationship. When you feel respected, you are able to be your genuine imperfect self in your relationship and are more likely to act respectfully to your partner. I am sure if I had met you at the beginning of your relationship you would have told me many things that you admired and respected about your partner. Unfortunately, over time, you and your partner might have started focusing on each other's weaknesses, or the traits you found annoying, and unknowingly begun to lose respect for each other.

All too often disrespect is communicated non-verbally through gestures, body language, tone of voice and attitude. One partner may suddenly feel a negative vibe; many times the other denies this, resulting in great confusion. In a couple's session, it might look something like this: Susan says, "I was having trouble understanding the directions, and when I asked you a question you were so short, glared, and grabbed the sheet from me." Then Michael responds, "I don't know what you're talking about. I was just trying to help, you're so sensitive all the time." I then notice that Susan is looking down, tearing up and I say, "Sue, what do you feel like at those moments when he's short with you?" She responds, "I just feel like a loser, then I get mad and wonder why I even bother asking him things." After a little processing and some gentle prodding, Michael admits, "I guess. . .sometimes at those moments, even though I would never say it to her, I do think. . .she's sort of stupid." Once we have all these emotional truths on the table we can begin to challenge those beliefs, explore how they have damaged the connection and work toward creating a more respectful relationship.

When you and your partner treat each other with respect and admiration, you reinforce the friendship, caring and connection in your relationship. The following conversation focuses on how you each experience respect in your relationship in order to create a firm foundation going forward.

Make a pot of tea or another soothing drink and find a comfortable quiet place to sit. Light a candle, give each other a hug and a smile and begin the next conversation.

Couple Conversation — 25
Respect

Take turns asking each other the following questions:

1. Do you feel safe to be your genuine, imperfect self with me?
2. Do I respect your suggestions?
3. Do I ever second-guess your decisions?
4. Do you feel like I have your back?
5. Am I ever rude to you?
6. Do I show you that I appreciate you?
7. Do you think that I take you seriously?
8. Do I treat you with as much respect now as I did early in our relationship?
9. Do I make you feel special?
10. Is there anything else I can do to show you more respect?

Now give each other a hug and a thank you for taking time to focus on each other and improve the connection in your relationship.

Clinician Prep — 26
Apologies and Forgiveness

1. Explain to your clients the importance of the following topic:

   "The topic of the twenty-sixth conversation you will have is 'Apologies. and Forgiveness'. In every relationship, there are times when feelings are hurt. Couples who are able to offer apologies and to forgive are able to endure and grow from those difficult experiences. Having a conversation about the importance of apologies and forgiveness will help you to create a more caring, compassionate and connected relationship."

2. Ask them each how connected they currently feel on a scale of 1-10.

   1_____10

3. Review the ritual they will create: "At the same time each day, make a pot of tea or another soothing drink and find a comfortable quiet place to sit. Light a candle, give each other a hug and a smile and begin the twenty-sixth conversation."

4. Explain that they will begin the twenty-sixth conversation by reading together the first page of the assignment and then begin the following conversation by taking turns asking each other the 10 questions.

5. Remind them to be open, respectful and non-judgmental.

6. Give them a copy of the following pages for Conversation #26 "Apologies and Forgiveness."

7. At the following session you will process:
   • how easy or difficult it was to create and follow the daily ritual
   • how it felt to share their answers
   • whether anything was particularly difficult to discuss
   • what they learned about themselves and each other

   And once again ask them each how connected they feel on a scale of 1-10.

   1_____10

Finally, thank the couple for taking time to focus on each other and improve the connection in their relationship.

I See You, You Matter, I Love You

"The heart that knows how to bow down and say sorry is the heart that loves the most."

Nishan Punwar

Regardless of how mindful and caring you are in your relationship, you will hurt and be hurt by one another at some point along the way. A relationship injury can be as subtle as not noticing when your partner has had a hard day and needs a hug, or as overt as forgetting your anniversary. You may be someone who naturally shows compassion and remorse for hurting your partner or you may instead quickly jump into a defensive mode finding excuses for your behavior, which ultimately invalidates your partner's feelings.

The ability to apologize and forgive is crucial in a relationship. Unfortunately, some people think that apologizing means they are admitting that they are inferior and weak and therefore choose to dig their feet in and dismiss their partner's feelings. If you take this approach, you will only hurt your partner and harm the connection in your relationship. It's important to understand that an apology is not an act of submission but an act of caring. Taking accountability for your actions or lack thereof and communicating to your partner that, "I see that you were hurt by my actions and that matters to me," is an incredibly caring gesture that validates your partner's feelings and helps get your relationship back on the path to connection.

In turn, forgiveness requires a decision to let go of resentment and any thought of revenge. You may find this very difficult to do, as you might believe it minimizes the hurt you experienced. It will help if you can see it instead as a tool to release the grip that hurt and anger have on you so that you can move forward in the relationship. Hanging onto anger creates resentment in the relationship and also chips away at the connection you have. Seeing forgiveness not as passive acceptance of the hurt you've experienced, but as an active effort to see us all as flawed human beings, will allow you to have compassion for your partner while also holding them accountable.

I have seen couples in my practice who have experienced great pain in the relationship and were able to heal over time through a combination of apologies and forgiveness. The following conversation focuses on your ability to apologize and forgive and how to make it easier for you to do so going forward.

Make a pot of tea or another soothing drink and find a comfortable quiet place to sit. Light a candle, give each other a hug and a smile and begin the next conversation.

Apologies and Forgiveness

Take turns asking each other the following questions:

1. Do you see apologizing as acting weak or inferior?
2. Were your parents able to apologize to you?
3. Did you ever see your parents apologize and forgive each other?
4. Has there been a time in our relationship when I have hurt you and not offered you an apology you needed?
5. Do you think it is compassionate to forgive others?
6. Do you think it is possible to hold others accountable and still forgive them?
7. If you apologized to your parents were they able to forgive you?
8. Do you think I am a forgiving person?
9. Is there anything that you feel I haven't forgiven you for?
10. Is there anything that I can do to make it easier for you to apologize or to forgive?

Now give each other a hug and a thank you for taking time to focus on each other and improve the connection in your relationship.

1. Explain to your clients the importance of the following topic:

   "The topic of the twenty-seventh conversation you will have is 'Challenges, Setbacks and Loss'. In your relationship there will be times when one of you experiences a challenge, setback or loss that cannot be healed or remedied by the other and instead what you will need is for your partner to be non-judgmental, supportive and empathic. Having a conversation about struggles you have had or are having and how you relate to each other at those times, will help you to be better partners and to feel more validated, cared for and connected then and always."

2. Ask them each how connected they currently feel on a scale of 1-10.

   1_____10

3. Review the ritual they will create: "At the same time each day, make a pot of tea or another soothing drink and find a comfortable quiet place to sit. Light a candle, give each other a hug and a smile and begin the twenty-seventh conversation."

4. Explain that they will begin the twenty-seventh conversation by reading together the first page of the assignment and then begin the following conversation by taking turns asking each other the 10 questions.

5. Remind them to be open, respectful and non-judgmental.

6. Give them a copy of the following pages for Conversation #27 "Challenges, Setbacks. and Loss."

7. At the following session you will process:
   • how easy or difficult it was to create and follow the daily ritual
   • how it felt to share their answers
   • whether anything was particularly difficult to discuss
   • what they learned about themselves and each other

   And once again ask them each how connected they feel on a scale of 1-10.

   1_____10

Finally, thank the couple for taking time to focus on each other and improve the connection in their relationship.

Couple Conversation — 27
Challenges, Setbacks and Loss

Life Brings Joy, Life Brings Suffering

"We are never so defenseless against suffering as when we love."

Sigmund Freud

Despite our best efforts to avoid them, we will all experience challenges, setbacks and loss in our lives. There are many different kinds of loss. Over the course of our lifetime we may experience loss of financial stability, jobs, homes, identity, health, dreams, friends and of course, the most acute loss and grief--when a loved one dies. We also grieve the loss of seemingly simple things in our lives. You may have experienced grief when saying goodbye to an old home as you moved to a new home in a new neighborhood, watched one season pass as a new one began, or at the end of a school year when a new one started. You may have grieved the loss of past chapters in your life as you transitioned to new stages; self-focused teenager to responsible young adult, carefree newlyweds to new parents, parents of adolescents to empty-nesters. You may even find you will grieve the loss of your young, healthy body as you age, slow down or possibly wrestle with illness.

It is vital to your relationship that you can trust your partner to be there to support you when you feel the fear, sadness and anxiety that can result from the challenges, setbacks and loss that life delivers. I have witnessed in my practice the devastation that can result when one partner struggles with a personal crisis and the other is unwilling or unable to emotionally support him or her. The subsequent sense of loneliness and abandonment often severs the connection in the relationship, and it cannot always be repaired.

As I'm sure you know, you often cannot solve your partner's problems, or heal their pain, but you can be there to listen to them, love them, validate their feelings and offer them emotional support. In the end that will deepen your connection and open a path to healing. The following conversation focuses on addressing any challenges, setbacks or loss you have experienced or are experiencing now and how you can be emotionally supportive of each other in the future.

Make a pot of tea or another soothing drink and find a comfortable quiet place to sit. Light a candle, give each other a hug and a smile and begin the next conversation.

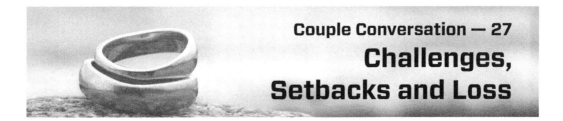

Couple Conversation — 27
Challenges, Setbacks and Loss

Take turns asking each other the following questions:

1. What is your first memory of loss, large or small?

2. Were you comforted by anyone?

3. What challenges did your family experience while you were growing up?

4. How did your parents cope with the challenges?

5. Have there been any especially difficult transitional times in your life so far?

6. Are you experiencing any challenges, setbacks or fears now?

7. When you are having a difficult time am I a good listener and do you feel validated and supported?

8. Is there a time when I could have been more supportive of you?

9. Do you feel comfortable listening to and being supportive of me when I am having difficulties?

10. Is there anything we can do as a couple to cope better with challenges, setbacks and loss in our life?

Now give each other a hug and a thank you for taking time to focus on each other and improve the connection in your relationship.

Clinician Prep — 28
Relationship Savings Account

1. Explain to your clients the importance of the following topic:

   "The topic of the twenty-eighth conversation you will have is 'Relationship Savings Account'. This refers to the buffer of positive feelings you create in your relationship that allows you to handle conflict without becoming negative, resentful and depleted. Having a conversation about how often you make deposits into your relationship savings account will help you to create ways to grow it going forward and ensure you have a nice solid buffer."

2. Ask them each how connected they currently feel on a scale of 1-10.

   1_____10

3. Review the ritual they will create: "At the same time each day, make a pot of tea or another soothing drink and find a comfortable quiet place to sit. Light a candle, give each other a hug and a smile and begin the twenty-eighth conversation."

4. Explain that they will begin the twenty-eighth conversation by reading together the first page of the assignment and then begin the following conversation by taking turns asking each other the questions.

5. Remind them to be open, respectful and non-judgmental.

6. Give them a copy of the following pages for Conversation #28 "Relationship Savings Account."

7. At the following session you will process:
   • how easy or difficult it was to create and follow the daily ritual
   • how it felt to share their answers
   • whether anything was particularly difficult to discuss
   • what they learned about themselves and each other

   And once again ask them each how connected they feel on a scale of 1-10.

   1_____10

Finally, thank the couple for taking time to focus on each other and improve the connection in their relationship.

Deposits vs. Withdrawals

*"Little kindnesses and courtesies are so important.
In relationships, the little things are the big things."*

Steven R. Covey

Just as having a financial savings account can buffer you from a rainy day, nurturing your relationship will create a healthy relationship savings account to buffer you from difficult times. The more caring and thoughtful things you do, the more you strengthen the positive feelings you have for each other. As a result, if you have an argument or are hurt or disappointed by each other, you will be much less likely to have automatic negative feelings or hold onto resentment.

In my couples therapy sessions, I often ask each partner what they have done lately to nurture the closeness and health of the relationship. Unfortunately, all too often, neither partner can think of anything focused specifically on the relationship. I then emphasize to them how simple kind words, actions and experiences go a long way to creating gratitude, connection and appreciation which in turn builds reserves in the relationship savings account.

It's important for you to know that simply spending time together doing household chores, running errands, cooking or sending a thoughtful text message during the day, can be just as beneficial as vacations, or celebrating birthdays and anniversaries. The following conversation focuses on the health of your relationship savings account currently and exploring ideas to grow it going forward.

Make a pot of tea or another soothing drink and find a comfortable quiet place to sit. Light a candle, give each other a hug and a smile and begin the next conversation.

Couple Conversation — 28
Relationship Savings Account

Take turns asking each other the following questions:

1. What things do I do that you would consider deposits into our relationship savings account?

2. Do you think I make these deposits often enough?

3. What would you say was the last withdrawal we made?

4. Do you think we make more deposits than withdrawals?

5. Do you think we spend enough time together just doing simple things like running errands?

6. Would you agree that it's important to say something nice to each other every day?

7. Do you like me to kiss you hello, goodbye, good-morning and goodnight?

8. What things do we do each week that nurture the positive feelings we have for each other?

9. When we have an argument are you able to remember the things you appreciate about me and our relationship?

10. What else can I do to increase our relationship savings account?

Now give each other a hug and a thank you for taking time to focus on each other and improve the connection in your relationship.

1. Explain to your clients the importance of the following topic:

   "The topic of the twenty-ninth conversation you will have is 'Our Life Path: Past, Present and Future'. Over the course of the previous conversations, you have learned a lot about the experiences and people that have shaped each of you, and now you will share the vision of your path going forward. Learning about how you each feel about growing older and what your dreams are, will allow you to create a meaningful and connected future together."

2. Ask them each how connected they currently feel on a scale of 1-10.

   1_____10

3. Review the ritual they will create: "At the same time each day, make a pot of tea or another soothing drink and find a comfortable quiet place to sit. Light a candle, give each other a hug and a smile and begin the twenty-ninth conversation."

4. Explain that they will begin the twenty-ninth conversation by reading together the first page of the assignment and then begin the following conversation by taking turns asking each other the 10 questions.

5. Remind them to be open, respectful and non-judgmental.

6. Give them a copy of the following pages for Conversation #29 "Our Life Path: Past, Present and Future."

7. At the following session you will process:
   • how easy or difficult it was to create and follow the daily ritual
   • how it felt to share their answers
   • whether anything was particularly difficult to discuss
   • what they learned about themselves and each other

   And once again ask them each how connected they feel on a scale of 1-10.

   1_____10

Finally, thank the couple for taking time to focus on each other and improve the connection in their relationship.

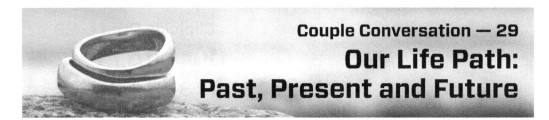

Dream a Little Dream with Me

"Whatever you can do, or dream you can, begin it. Boldness has genius, power and magic in it."

Johann Wolfgang Von Goethe

Neither of you grew up alone on an island. As we've covered, from the moment you were born, you interacted verbally and non-verbally with your parents, family and the outside world. These interactions began to form your view of yourself and the world around you and this view became the lens and filter through which you saw and experienced your life. As you ventured out into the world, interactions with others in your community and the larger society continued to shape your life view and self-image. You were affected by experiences in and out of your control and these experiences created the shape, texture and feelings along your life path.

Understanding how your partner's life experiences has impacted the way they think and feel helps you to be more respectful of them and their point of view and more open to their influence in the relationship. I have experienced many beautiful moments in sessions when each partner listens intently to the other sharing of his or her life story and then expressing how much more they understand one another and how much closer they feel. Awareness of how each of your pasts impacts your present helps you to feel more connected to each other and helps you visualize your future path together.

If you and your partner have a strong sense of shared goals and meaning in your life you will experience a greater sense of connection in the relationship. You will then find that you share an appreciation for your life path in the present and enjoy talking about and making plans for your future together. The following conversation focuses on examining your journeys so far and visualizing the future you want to create together.

Make a pot of tea or another soothing drink and find a comfortable quiet place to sit. Light a candle, give each other a hug and a smile and begin the next conversation.

Couple Conversation — 29
Our Life Path:
Past, Present and Future

Take turns asking each other the following questions:

1. What were some of the happiest times in your childhood?

2. Were there any difficult experiences that you think shaped who you are today?

3. Does the life you have now look like the life you envisioned when you were growing up?

4. How would you define a successful life?

5. What would you say is your purpose in life?

6. What makes your life meaningful?

7. How do you feel about getting older?

8. What are some of your dreams for the future?

9. Do you think it's important for us to have some shared dreams and goals?

10. How can I help you achieve your dreams?

Now give each other a hug and a thank you for taking time to focus on each other and improve the connection in your relationship.

Clinician Prep — 30
Keeping Connected

1. Explain to your clients the importance of the following topic:

   "Congratulations, you have reached the thirtieth and last conversation. The topic is 'Keeping Connected,' and during this conversation you will review the topics you discussed throughout the book, what you learned about yourself and each other and the impact this experience has had on your relationship."

2. Ask them each how connected they currently feel on a scale of 1-10.

   1———————————————————————10

3. Review the ritual they will create: "As you have each day, make a pot of tea or another soothing drink and find a comfortable quiet place to sit. Light a candle, give each other a hug and a smile and begin the thirtieth and last conversation."

4. Explain that they will begin the thirtieth conversation by reading together the first page of the assignment and then begin the following conversation by taking turns asking each other the 10 questions.

5. Remind them to be open, respectful and non-judgmental.

6. Give them a copy of the following pages for Conversation #30 "Keeping Connected."

7. At the following session:
   - review their answers to each of the 10 questions.
   - thank them for allowing you to share this process with them!
   - encourage them to continue the daily connection ritual!
   - give them a copy of the "couples therapy workbook booster session" to complete in a month and then periodically thereafter and review it with them in the following sessions.

   And once again ask them each how connected they feel on a scale of 1-10.

   1———————————————————————10

Finally, thank the couple for taking time to focus on each other and improve the connection in their relationship.

Couple Conversation — 30
Keeping Connected

Feeling Love, Accepting Love, Showing Love

"Only through our connectedness to others can we really know and enhance the self.
And only through working on the self can we begin to enhance our connectedness to others."

Harriet Goldhor Lerner

Congratulations you have reached the thirtieth conversation. For some of you this may be day 30, while others may have reached this conversation after several months. As I mentioned at the beginning of the book, this was not to be a race but a journey. You most likely discovered along the way that this journey was multi-layered. The first layer was educational and, hopefully, it allowed you to learn a great deal about important aspects of personal and relationship growth. The next layer was the experience of making time together a priority and having meaningful conversations, and I hope you learned to enjoy that. The third layer was that of learning about each other's personal history and how it relates to your current experience with many aspects of life. Finally, there was the layer of learning to be present and focused in order to really connect with each other.

I hope you learned the importance of nurturing the friendship, the affection, the romance and the physical and emotional intimacy in your relationship. I hope you have a greater understanding of how you were each affected by your family of origin, who your greatest influences were and what struggles you have had with self-esteem, grief, loss and setbacks. I hope you have a greater understanding of how and why you have conflict, what your defense mechanisms are, what your assumptions about yourself and your partner are and which steps of the dance that you do together work for you and which need to change. I hope you addressed what you need to do to trust and feel safe, how to communicate so that you are heard and to listen so that your partner feels heard and what your idea of fidelity and boundaries are. I hope that you have learned the importance of creating rituals, being present and showing that you appreciate and care for each other in order to make continuous deposits into the relationship savings account. And, finally, I hope that you are more able to accept and appreciate each other, to experience empathy, respect, joy and gratitude, to share a vision of your life goals and dreams and always to remember what it was like to fall in love with each other. And mostly I hope that all of this new awareness and time spent together has resulted in a greater sense of connection and a desire to nurture that connection day after day after day. . .until death do you part.

The last conversation of "Couples Therapy Workbook: Guided Relationship-Building Conversations" focuses on sharing what you have each learned on this journey together!

Make a pot of tea or another soothing drink and find a comfortable quiet place to sit. Light a candle, give each other a hug and a smile and begin the last conversation.

Couple Conversation — 30
Keeping Connected

And now, one final assignment to share what you learned on this journey. Be *present* and *listen with intention* as you take turns answering the following questions out loud.

1. When we first began this book I felt. . .

2. The topics that were the most interesting to me were. . .

3. The topics that were the most difficult to discuss were. . .

4. The topics I found we were the most alike on were. . .

5. The topics we differed the most on were. . .

6. The most important things I learned about myself were. . .

7. The most important things I learned about you were. . .

8. The most important things I learned about our relationship were. . .

9. The impact this experience has had on our relationship is. . .

10. In order to continue on this healthy, intimate and connected relationship path I will return to this book in a month and periodically thereafter to do the **Couples Therapy Workbook Booster Session** with you, and I will . . .

Once again give each other a hug and a thank you for taking the time to focus on each other and improve the connection in your relationship. I wish you well as you continue on your own unique relationship journey.

Booster Session

Hello again and welcome back. Whether this is your first Booster Session or your tenth, I hope you enjoy revisiting the topics of the many conversations you had with your partner during the "Couples Therapy Workbook" and noting the improvements you have made to your relationship since then.

Once again, make a pot of tea or another soothing drink and find a comfortable quiet place to sit. Light a candle, give each other a hug and a smile and begin the Booster Session.

Be present and listen with intention as you take turns answering the following questions out loud.

1. The things that I have done to improve the friendship in our relationship are. . .
2. I have made efforts to show you more caring and affection by. . .
3. The rituals I have really enjoyed are. . .
4. I have tried to improve our communication by. . .
5. I have tried to be more respectful when we are in conflict by. . .
6. The deposits I have made to our "relationship savings account" are. . .
7. I have nurtured the emotional and sexual intimacy in our relationship by. . .
8. When you have had challenges lately I have been supportive by...
9. Since completing "Couples Therapy Workbook" I have been grateful for. . .
10. Is there anything else you would like from me to improve the connection in our relationship?

Once again give each other a hug and a thank you for taking the time to focus on each other and improve the connection in your relationship. I commend you for valuing your relationship enough to have periodic Booster Sessions and encourage you to keep it up.

Bibliography and Further Reading
Values, Spirituality, Fidelity & Grief

Hayes, S.C., & Smith, S. (2005). *Get Out of Your Mind & Into Your Life: The New Acceptance & Commitment Therapy.* Oakland: New Harbinger.

Kubler-Ross, E., & Kessler, D. (2000). *Life Lessons: Two Experts on Death and Dying Teach Us About the Mysteries of Life and Living.* New York: Scribner.

Ruiz, D.M. (1999). *The Mastery of Love.* San Raphael: Amber-Allen Publishing Inc.

Spring, J.A., & Spring, M. (1996). *After the Affair: Healing the Pain and Rebuilding Trust When a Partner Has Been Unfaithful.* New York: Harper.

Tolle, E. (2005). *A New Earth: Awakening to Your Life's Purpose.* New York: Penguin Group.

Parenting & Family

Carter, B., & McGoldrick, M. (1999). *The Expanded Family Life Cycle, 3rd edition.* Needham Heights: Allyn & Bacon.

Ricker, A., Calmes, R.E., &Sneyd, L.W. (2006). *How Happy Families Happen.* Center City: Hazelden.

Yerkovich, M., & Yerkovich, K. (2011). *How We Love Our Kids.* Colorado Springs: Waterbrook Press.

Communication

Beck, J.S., (1995). *Cognitive Therapy: Basics and Beyond.* New York: The Guilford Press.

Evans, P., (2010). *The Verbally Abusive Relationship, 3rd edition.* Avon: Adams Media.

Keirsey, D. (1998). *Please Understand Me II: Temperament Character Intelligence.* Del Mar: Prometheus Nemesis Book Company.

Lerner, H. (1989). *The Dance of Intimacy: A Woman's Guide To Courageous Acts of Change In Key Relationships.* New York: Harper & Row, Publishers Inc.

McKay, M., Fanning, P., & Paleg, K. (2006). *Couple Skills: Making Your Relationship Work, 2nd edition.* Oakland: New Harbinger.

Romance, Connection & Attachment

Chapman, G. (2004). *The Five Love Languages: How to Express Heartfelt Commitment to Your Mate.* Chicago: Northfield Publishing.

Fisher, H. (1992). *Anatomy of Love.* New York: The Random House Publishing Group.

Gottman, J.M., & Silver, N. (1999). *The Seven Principles For Making Marriage Work.* New York: Three Rivers Press.

Goulston, M.D., & Goldberg, P. (2001). *The 6 Secrets of a Lasting Relationship: How to Fall in Love Again – and Stay There.* New York: Penguin Group Inc.

Hendrix, H. & Hunt, H.L. (2008). *Getting The Love You Want: A Guide For Couples.* New York: Henry Holt and Company, LLC.

Johnson. S. (2008). *Hold Me Tight: Seven Conversations for a Lifetime Love.* New York: Little, Brown and Company.

Johnson, S.M. (1996). *The Practice of Emotionally Focused Marital Therapy: Creating Connection.* Philadelphia: Brunner/Mazel.

Lerner, H. (2001). *The Dance of Connection.* New York: Harper Collins Publishers.

McCarthy, B.W., & McCarthy, E. (2009). *Discovering Your Couple Sexual Style.* New York: Routledge.

Real, T. (2007). *The New Rules of Marriage: What You Need To Know To Make Love Work.* New York: Ballantine Books.

Yerkovich, M., & Yerkovich, K. (2008). *How We Love.* Colorado Springs: Waterbrook Press.